MY COMPANION
THROUGH GRIEF

MY COMPANION THROUGH GRIEF

Comfort for Your Darkest Hours

GARY D. KINNAMAN

Regal

From Gospel Light
Ventura, California, U.S.A.

PUBLISHED BY REGAL BOOKS
FROM GOSPEL LIGHT
VENTURA, CALIFORNIA, U.S.A.
PRINTED IN THE U.S.A.

Regal Books is a ministry of Gospel Light, a Christian publisher dedicated to serving the local church. We believe God's vision for Gospel Light is to provide church leaders with biblical, user-friendly materials that will help them evangelize, disciple and minister to children, youth and families.

It is our prayer that this Regal book will help you discover biblical truth for your own life and help you meet the needs of others. May God richly bless you.

For a free catalog of resources from Regal Books/Gospel Light, please call your Christian supplier or contact us at 1-800-4-GOSPEL *or* www.regalbooks.com.

Rights for publishing this book in other languages are contracted by Gospel Light Worldwide, the international nonprofit ministry of Gospel Light. Gospel Light Worldwide also provides publishing and technical assistance to international publishers dedicated to producing Sunday School and Vacation Bible School curricula and books in the languages of the world. For additional information, visit www.gospellightworldwide.org; write to Gospel Light Worldwide, P.O. Box 3875, Ventura, CA 93006; or send an e-mail to info@gospellightworldwide.org.

In loving memory

BOBBIE BEADLE
January 1988-December 1988

MATTHEW BUCKLEY
1975-1992

BILL DALTON
1961-1976
WENDY DALTON
1962-1963
TOM DALTON
1964-1983

MARLIN DAVIS, JR.
1967-1987
EDDIE DAVIS
1970-1987
MATTHEW DAVIS
1972-1987

ERIC EDWARDS
1973-1991

ROBERT HAWK
1960-1988

LANE LAWSON
1967-1994

DANIEL MURROW
1977-1994

JACK STEVENS
1955-1986

And with inexpressible gratitude to their families....
Their grief was the dark womb of this book.

Contents

Acknowledgments

I am profoundly grateful for the people who have shared with me their personal stories and insights about grief. Without them, this book would not have been possible: John and Margie Dalton, Mark and Christina Buckley, Judy Hawk, Paul and Debbi Edwards, Leroy Lawson, David Murrow, and Mary Beth Roosa—to whose loved ones I have dedicated this book. Their enormous loss has been our great gain.

Thank you to the many other people who allowed me to share small slices of their lives. Some of the names and details of their stories have been changed to protect their anonymity.

I would also like to acknowledge, with special appreciation, all the helpful people at Servant Publications, especially Bert Ghezzi, for coming up with the original idea for this book and for being such an encouragement to me personally; Al Lukaszewski, a student at Fuller Seminary and a part-time librarian, who helped me recover bibliographical information when my computer crashed. And thanks to Gwen Ellis, who skillfully edited the manuscript.

Thanks also to the staff and congregation of Word of Grace Church, whom I have served as senior minister for fourteen years and who have shared my time with all of you who read this book.

Introduction

If you are going through a time of loss and grief, you may or may not read all of this book. It's probably hard for you to read anything. It's probably hard for you just to think.

That's why this book is designed the way it is. I've worked hard to make it easy to read. But I've also made every effort to challenge your thinking and stir your emotions.

You can also see that this book is formatted to allow you to read bits and pieces. Thoughtful quotations, Bible verses, excerpts from well-known Christian writers, and sensitive and empathetic personal stories are interwoven throughout the text. In some places I've put Scripture in bold type to emphasize its importance. Please be aware that emphasis is mine.

We've purposefully titled this book *My Companion through Grief.* We want it to be your friend. I've prayed, and my church has prayed, that when you read it, God himself will speak to you.

ONE

More Questions Than Answers
Discovering the Depth of God's Grace

With the death of every friend I love, a part of me has been buried, but their contribution to my being of happiness, strength, and understanding remains to sustain me in an altered world.

HELEN KELLER

For men are not cast off by the Lord forever. Though he brings grief, he will show compassion, so great is his unfailing love. For he does not willingly bring affliction or grief to the children of men. LAMENTATIONS 3:31-33

I've never lost a child. My parents are still living. I have two brothers, both alive and well. I haven't even lost a nephew or niece.

We came real close to it when my brother's little boy was diagnosed with a life-threatening brain tumor lodged a microscopic distance from his brain stem, and growing larger by the day. I'll never forget the suffocating fear that silenced our whole family.

As I knelt by Alan's hospital bed, I tried to pray. All I could do was cry. "That kind of tumor is always malignant," a radiologist friend told me. But amazingly and miraculously it wasn't, and years later Alan's only reminder of his brush with death is a nasty scar, protruding ever so slightly below the hairline on the back of his neck.

Other families have not been so fortunate. In my role of pastor for nearly twenty-five years, I've walked with countless people through the valley of the shadow of death. "Normal" death, as in the case of an elderly person dying, is hard enough to take. At this moment, as I write, my mother is watching her own mother's life slowly slipping away. Not too long ago, I watched an elderly gentleman awkwardly lean his aged body over the open casket of his wife of sixty years. Tenderly he whispered in her cold ear, "Good-bye, Dear. See you in heaven." I lost it. I've conducted scores of funerals, but this one made me as sad as any.

OUTRAGEOUSLY TRAGIC DEATH

Though mortals, a vestige of God's original creation in each of us believes that death was never really meant to happen, especially outrageously tragic death, like when a deeply committed Christian family lost three of their five children in one day. While their oldest son was flying their private plane, it stalled and crashed. His two brothers and another friend were on board. No one survived.

At the funeral, friends of the family and a parade of sobbing teenagers rolled three caskets down the center aisle of the church. I still can't believe the whole thing happened. It was surreal. But the immediate family, much to my surprise, seemed to be handling their incomprehensible loss unusually well. The presiding pastor had a wonderful message, and it really seemed like God was going to pull them through. But within a couple of years, because of their over-whelming grief and their inability to deal with such an enormous tragedy, the calamity was compounded when the parents' marriage dissolved, something that is not uncommon in families who have lost children. Yes, grief is that difficult.

When God Slams the Door

Meanwhile, where is God? This is one of the disquieting symptoms. When you are happy, so happy that you have no sense of needing Him, so happy that you are tempted to feel his claims upon you as an interruption, if you remember yourself and turn to Him with gratitude and praise, you will be—or so it feels—welcomed with open arms. But go to Him when your need is desperate, when all other help is vain, and what do you find? A door slammed in your face, and a sound of bolting and double bolting on the inside. After that, silence. You may as well turn away. The longer you wait, the more emphatic the silence will become. There are no lights in the windows. It might be an empty house. Was it ever inhabited? It seemed so once. And that seeming was as strong as this. What can this mean? Why is He so present a commander in our time of prosperity and so very absent a help in time of trouble?

C.S. Lewis[1]

Five years later, almost to the day, the mother of those three boys was sitting in my office. I can still see her lovely, lonely face. Her eyes were dry, but she wasn't over the pain. Her piercing eyes searched my face, hoping for some impartation of heavenly wisdom. I was speechless, except for small talk.

Her eyes drifted away, perhaps to some distant memory, as she acknowledged, "You know, God has been taking care of me in unusual ways since the accident. I've seen his hand working in my life." I could detect genuine gratefulness. "But his provision has been bittersweet," she confessed, with a touch of cynicism. "I've often wondered why he's taken such good care of me *after* letting my children die."

I agreed it was cruel irony. For a moment I wondered if maybe God felt bad about the whole thing himself. Maybe he was just trying to make it up to her.

Some suffering is so extraordinary that even the most godly people have doubts about whether or not God really cares about them, or even if there is a God. Even Jesus was heard to cry, "My God, My God, why have you forsaken me?"[2]

Prayer of the Forsaken

To come to the pleasure you have not you must go by a way in which you enjoy not.
ST. JOHN OF THE CROSS

There is no more plaintive or heartfelt prayer than the cry of Jesus: "My God, my God, why hast thou forsaken me?"
MATTHEW 27:46B, KJV

Jesus' experience on the cross was, of course, utterly unique and unrepeatable, for he took into himself the sin of the world. But in our own way you and I *will* pray the Prayer of the Forsaken if we seek the intimacy of perpetual communion with the Father. Times of seeming desertion and absence and abandonment appear to be universal among those who have walked this path of faith before us. We might just as well get used to the idea that, sooner or later, we, too, will know what it means to feel forsaken by God.

The old writers spoke of this reality as *Deus Absconditus*—the God who is hidden. Almost instinctively you understand the experience they were describing, don't you? Have you ever tried to pray and felt nothing, seen nothing, sensed nothing? Has it ever seemed as if your prayers did no more than bounce off the ceiling and ricochet around an empty room? Have there been times when you desperately needed some word of assurance, some demonstration of divine presence, and you got nothing? Sometimes it just seems like God is hidden from us. We do everything we know to do. We pray; we serve; we worship. We live as faithfully as we can. And there is still nothing... nothing! It feels like we are "beating on Heaven's door with bruised knuckles in the dark," to use the words of George Buttrick.

I am sure you understand that when I speak of the absence of God, I am talking about a *sense* of absence. God is always present with us—we know that theologically—but there are times when he withdraws our consciousness of his presence.

But these theological niceties are of little help to us when we enter the Sahara of the heart. Here we experience real spiritual desolation. We feel abandoned by friends, spouse, and God. Every hope evaporates the moment we reach for it. Every dream dies the moment we try to realize it. We question, we doubt, we struggle. Nothing helps. We pray and the words seem empty. We turn to the Bible and find it meaningless. We turn to music and it fails to move us. We seek the fellowship of other Christians and discover only backbiting, selfishness, and egoism.

The biblical metaphor for these experiences of forsakenness is the desert. It is an apt image, for we do indeed feel dry, barren, parched. With the psalmist we cry out, "O my God, I cry out by day, but you do not answer, by night, and am not silent" (Psalm 22:2). In fact, we begin to wonder if there is a God to answer.

These experiences of abandonment and desertion have come and will come to us all.

> *God, Where Are You? What have I done to make you hide from me? Are you playing cat and mouse with me, or are your purposes larger than my perceptions? I feel alone, lost, forsaken.*
>
> RICHARD FOSTER[3]

Nine years ago, a local fire captain was killed in a horrific traffic accident. His engine company was on a routine run to another station. A fully loaded concrete truck, heading for the same intersection, never saw him. Jack left behind four children and his wife, Mary Beth.

"Thank you," Mary Beth wrote to me, "for giving me the opportunity to share about my experience with grief for your book. I found, however, that even though it has been nine years since Jack died, and I have a wonderful new husband and new life, I cannot revisit that time of my life without still experiencing tremendous pain.… Maybe some day, after my children are grown, I will be able to go back and perhaps write my own book."

And here's that cruel irony again: she adds, "I will never forget how the Lord walked beside me. He was closer at that time than ever before or after. It is forever etched in my memory and heart." Perhaps Jeremiah had this irony in mind when he wrote,

> Though he brings grief, he will show compassion,
> so great is his unfailing love.
> For he does not willingly bring affliction
> or grief to the children of men.…
>
> Is it not from the mouth of the Most High
> that both calamities and good things come?
>
> LAMENTATIONS 3:32, 33, 38

How long will the healing take? For Mary Beth, *at least* ten years. Sometimes a lifetime isn't quite long enough.

A woman in her sixties, whom I thought I knew fairly well, told me about the dark shadow that fell across her younger years. (Oh, the secret sufferings your friends never share!) I had asked her innocently about her family. She told me how, many years ago, her little daughter was playing in their driveway on a happy, sunny day. Unnoticed by a friend who was backing her car into the street, the child was killed instantly. Time alone doesn't heal, because forty years later the memory still filled her mommy's eyes with tears.

At some point your grief will end, but this doesn't mean that there will ever be an end to your sense of loss.

HELEN FITZGERALD[4]

Misery's Shadow...

Part of every misery is, so to speak, the misery's shadow or reflection: the fact that you don't merely suffer but have to keep on thinking about the fact that you suffer. I not only live each endless day in grief, but live each day thinking about living each day in grief.... There is nothing we can do with the suffering except to suffer it. Who still thinks there is some device (if only he could find it) which will make pain not to be pain. It doesn't really matter whether you grip the arms of the dentist's chair or let your hands lie in your lap. The drill drills on.... What do people mean when they say, "I am not afraid of God because I know He is good"? Have they never been to the dentist?

C.S. LEWIS[5]

Every imaginable evil lurks just around the corner of life's mean streets. Like death. And divorce. And miscarriages. And debilitating illnesses. And broken relationships. And the loss of a job or career. Just moments before I began writing this chapter, an E-mail message flashed across my computer screen.

A close friend, whose marriage of many years had recently ended, called our office for more prayer. His daughter had run away, but fortunately was found, and she's OK. His other daughter totaled his car, so he's without a vehicle, except for his company car, which isn't supposed to be used for personal business. The sterile, electronic message ended, "He needs a financial miracle." I prayed the best I could. Helplessly.

Lord, Hear Me in My Distress...

Sometimes I don't even know how to pray for myself. This year, God has given our church enormous success. At least that's what all the right numbers tell us. Am I happy? I'm profoundly honored that God would show us such favor, but I've never had more anxiety in my life! Psalm 20 has been a lifeline. Read it thoughtfully, with your heart open to the Holy Spirit:

> May the Lord answer you **when you are in distress;**
> may the name of the God of Jacob protect you.
> May he send you help from the sanctuary
> and grant you support from Zion.
> **May he remember all your sacrifices**
> **and accept your burnt offerings.**
> **Selah** [Think about it!] Psalms 20:1-3

I've made so many sacrifices through the years. For my family. For the church. For God! But my sacrifices, all of them, are tarnished. Only the sacrifice of Jesus, the Lamb without spot or blemish, is completely acceptable to God. And I am not even slightly persuaded that one or more of my sacrifices has contributed in any way to my eternal salvation, which remains an unmerited gift of God's incredible grace. But Psalm 20 has brought me lasting encouragement, because I know from God's Word that he will not forget what I've done in service for him.

The psalmist continues:

> May he give you the desire of your heart
> and make all your plans succeed.
> We will shout for joy when you are victorious
> and will lift up our banners in the name of our God.
> May the Lord grant all your requests.
> Now I know that the Lord saves his anointed;
> he answers him from his holy heaven
> with the saving power of his right hand.
> Some trust in chariots and some in horses,
> but we trust in the name of our God.

They are brought to their knees and fall,
but we rise up and stand firm.
O Lord, save the king!
Answer us when we call! PSALMS 20:4-9

Like a prescription of spiritual medication, Psalm 20 has been sustaining me. I've read this passage over and over. God's Word really is a lamp to my feet and a light for the pathways of my darkest nights.

How is it that the Bible has such power in people's lives? Years ago I met Christian author and living martyr Richard Wurmbrand, who was first tortured as a prisoner of the Nazis for being Jewish and later tortured as a prisoner of the Romanian Communists for being a Christian. He likes to tell about how many people have asked him, "What Bible verse sustained you when you were in prison?"

"No Bible verse sustained me," is his perplexing reply, to which he adds (after pausing for effect!), "The *God* of the Bible sustained me."

This is why the Bible "works." It's not just a wonderful collection of religious stories and spiritual insights. It's God's book. It's God-breathed. The Word of God is a means of grace. When God speaks, his Word carries his healing presence. I think this is something of what the apostle Paul meant when he wrote:

I was given the gift of a handicap to keep me in constant touch with my limitations. Satan's angel did his best to get me down; what he in fact did was push me to my knees... At first I didn't think of it as a gift, and begged God to remove it. Three times I did that, and then he told me,
"My grace is enough; it's all you need.
My strength comes into its own in your weakness."
Once I heard that, I was glad to let it happen. I quit focusing on the handicap and began appreciating the gift. It was a case of Christ's strength moving in my weakness. Now I take limitations

in stride, and with good cheer, these limitations that cut me down to size—abuse, accidents, opposition, bad breaks. I just let Christ take over! And so the weaker I get, the stronger I become.

2 CORINTHIANS 12:7-10, *THE MESSAGE*[6]

Probably without thinking specifically about this verse, Mary Beth, within weeks after the death of her fire-fighter husband, penned this lovely praise to God:

Such Grace!

Oh, the love of the Lord in a dry and empty place!
Never before have I tasted such grace.
Though pain overwhelm me,
Though sorrow increase,
Under His wings there is eternal peace.

Oh, what a mystery! How can this be?
Beneath such despair there is tranquility.
Within my own weakness His strength is divine.
I would have perished if Jesus weren't mine.

—Mary Beth Roosa

Shortly after I agreed to write this book, I met John and Margie Dalton and stayed in their home for a few days. I have to believe it was Providence, a divinely appointed resource for me. And for them, it was a divinely appointed opportunity to speak about their loss and grief. I'm a seminary graduate, but they're the real experts on this subject. You see, they've watched three children die: two of terminal illnesses and one suddenly, in a mountain climbing accident. Margie wrote to me:

NO ANSWERS, LOTS OF GRACE

There are times in our lives when we demand to know answers to the unanswerable; answers that only eternity will reveal to us. We do not understand truths hidden in the depths of eternity. We do not understand the love of God when tragedy strikes, or when children die. In a time of sorrow and grief it is difficult for us to comprehend that God is with us. That God's love, deeper than the deepest sea, could possibly still be surrounding us. That God in his love has allowed searing pain.

Now, as I reflect on our terrible loss, I am in awe of God's incredible grace. Grace to forgive when I have felt absolutely unable to forgive. Grace to restore us when restoration was beyond our wildest dreams. And grace to heal us. God's love for us has been extravagant. God's love pursued us when we were running from his presence. I actually feel honored God chose to prune us, to allow despair in our lives. Through it, God has brought us to understand that relationship with him, Abba Father, is the only thing that matters in our lives.

This book is not about easy answers, although it may help you find some meaning in your suffering and loss. Instead, this book is about empathy and comfort and healing. Above all, it's about finding God when life seems to have given you every reason to believe he doesn't care, or even that there is no God. This book is about God's Word and the mystery of his healing presence and grace in a terribly broken world. I have few things to say myself, but I've gathered the wisdom and thoughtful stories of dozens of Christian leaders and ordinary people like John and Margie, each of whom in his and her own way has found consolation in God's love and presence. When we suffer, we need more than answers; we need each other and we need God.

> Deep calls to deep
> In the roar of your waterfalls;
> all your waves and breakers
> have swept over me.
> By day the Lord directs his love,
> at night his song is with me—
> a prayer to the God of my life.
>
> I say to God my Rock,
> "Why have you forgotten me?

Why must I go about mourning,
oppressed by the enemy?"
My bones suffer mortal agony
as my foes taunt me,
saying to me all day long,
"Where is your God?"

Why are you downcast, O my soul?
Why so disturbed within me?
Put your hope in God,
for I will yet praise him,
my Savior and my God. PSALMS 42:7-11

PART ONE

GRIEF

Understanding Yourself

T W O

Does Grief Come in Stages?
Understanding Grief and Its Process

Each experience of grief is unique.

MADELEINE L'ENGLE

But with knowledge one can learn to do the necessary grief work, to carry out the task of mourning so that bereavement finally becomes not a burden, but a positive thing to help one grow in freedom.

ARTHUR FREESE

Grieving is hard. It need not be hellish.

ALLA RENÉE BOZARTH

Does anyone really understand human behavior? Lots of people have tried, pastors and psychologists among them. My son is majoring in psychology, and he probably thinks he's getting a handle on it, but give him a good dose of life, then we'll see.

I mean, when everything is going right, do you really understand why you feel what you feel? Or why you think what you think? Or do what you do? But add divorce, the loss of a job, death, or some other trauma into the mixture of your emotions, and you will confess with the apostle Paul, "If the power of sin within me keeps sabotaging my best intentions, I obviously need help!"

"I realize that I don't have what it takes," he laments. "I can will it, but I can't *do* it. I decide to do good, but I don't *really* do it; I decide not to do bad, but then I do it anyway…. Something has gone wrong deep within me and gets the better of me every time. It happens so regularly that it's predictable" (Romans 7:18-21, *The Message*).

It sounds like Paul is saying that the only thing that's predictable is his unpredictability, and we all know this is especially true when the pressure's on.

IT'S A JUNGLE IN THERE

"The experts" (who are not always the ones who are grieving) have identified "stages" of grief, which may sound as though you can work through your bereavement in an orderly way, like reading through the chapters of a book. Certainly, grief has distinct components, and we'll talk about those. But bereavement is probably the most complex, intense, and prolonged expression of human emotion. An exact science it isn't. Helen Fitzgerald, author of the wonderfully comprehensive *The Mourning Handbook*, calls grief "unlike other life experiences."[1]

It's a jungle in there. Everything inside you is savage and snarled. Screeching emotions and venomous attitudes. No trail in sight. And just when you thought tomorrow was the way out, everything gets overgrown again overnight.

William Stringfellow, a theologian and lawyer, writes about coping with the death of his son, defining this wilderness of grief as "the total experience of loss, anger, outrage, fear, regret, melancholy, abandonment, and temptation, suffered privately within one's self, in response to the happening of death."[2] Grief is immeasurably painful and complex.

But It Hurts...Differently

There's no way to predict
how you will feel.

The reactions of grief are
not like recipes,
with given ingredients,
and certain results.

Each person mourns in a
different way.

You may cry hysterically,
or
you may remain outwardly controlled,
showing little emotion.

You may lash out in anger against
your family and friends,
or
you may express your gratitude
for their dedication.

You may be calm one moment—
in turmoil the next.

Reactions are varied and
contradictory.

Grief is universal.
At the same time it
is extremely personal.

Heal in your own way.

EARL A. GROLLMAN[3]

John Dalton, Margie's husband and a Christian physician, wrote to me:

> My sense of grief is that it is a very long road traveled alone in the inner heart. Even describing grief as a journey is less than satisfactory, because I have not experienced grief in a linear dimension, going through defined stages of development so dear to the thinking of our culture. I might more accurately describe grief as a place where I may choose to allow entrance to no one, even my real person at times.

Even so, John admits that he and his wife have worked through their grief in three fairly definable seasons: acute pain, dull pain, and healing.

Season 1: Acute Pain

> The bereaved are caught in wild, uncontrollable crosscurrents of irrational and opposite feelings which come rolling over them in successive and unpredictable ways.
>
> ARTHUR FREESE[4]

Speaking as a grieving father, not a clinical expert, John Dalton refers to the first phase of the grieving process as a period of "acute, high, painful energy," which lasts about two months. This, he says, is the experience of intense grief, shock, severe emotional distress, anxiety, and fear. According to John, this is a time when people can even have feelings of malice and revenge, deeply rooted in lingering anger.

John's wife, Margie, wrote to me:

> John and I were in such pain that we had to turn away from one another. We couldn't bear to see each other in such grief. Many families become dysfunctional or even break apart after the death

of a child, and it has only been by the grace of God that our marriage has survived. Grief causes so much need within us that, avoiding those who are closest to us, we are inclined to turn toward others, or to work, or to exercise. Any*thing* to take our minds away from the cancerous agony. Any*one* but a spouse.

Children suffer in this environment, too, because we moms and dads cannot provide the answers—the love they need. Knowing how much I felt we had neglected our living children, I grieved for them as much as I did for the ones I had lost. I remember praying that God would bring others alongside to befriend and love our children.

> Be merciful to me, Lord, for I am faint;
> O Lord, heal me, for my bones are in agony.
> My soul is in anguish.
> How long, O Lord, how long?
>
> Turn, O Lord, and deliver me;
> save me because of your unfailing love.
> No one remembers you when he is dead.
> Who praises you from the grave?
>
> I am worn out from groaning;
> all night long I flood my bed with weeping
> and drench my couch with my tears.
> My eyes grow weak with sorrow. PSALMS 6:2-7

Season 2: Dull Pain

John describes the second phase in the grief process as a long period—months, years—of low energy, characterized by a lack of motivation and ambition, indifference, passivity, and unhealthy introversion. During this season of grief, when nothing really seems to matter, others will sense the loneliness and may even avoid the grieving person, which further seals him or her in isolation.

At this stage, even best friends, becoming impatient, will try to hurry the healing by encouraging the hurting person to be more energetic and active. They assume that grief is linear and are swayed by the myth that "It's time to get over it and move on." They are trying to help and do not realize that the helper has moved further along the path than the sufferer.

Judy Hawk, who lost her adult son in a terrible automobile accident, wrote to me:

> Through our experience of loss, my husband Lyle and I learned never to judge a person who is grieving. People close to us, we found, were concerned we were grieving too much or too long.
>
> Friends will want to help clean out your loved one's room and closets. They want you to get back into being busy. You will be told that you must go on with your life, forget the past, and find something worthwhile to get your troubled mind off the grief.
>
> I can't emphasize enough that people close to you have nothing but the best intentions. In fact, I used to be one of those people before I lost my son! But counsel from family and friends based on how they perceive the progress of your healing can be very hurtful during your season of loss.
>
> Unless a grieving person is clinically depressed, and in that case, virtually unable to help themselves, they should be allowed to work through their grief on their own—without a lot of well-meaning suggestions from caring friends. *Each person grieves differently.* I can't say that enough! Ultimately, healing from loss comes from the freedom to grieve at your own pace.

Having lunch today with a friend who lost her twenty-nine-year-old son five months ago, we found ourselves talking about what I have come to call "quick-fix friends." How, I wondered again, can family survivors let the world know how to help people wisely?

"Quick-fix people" are those friends and coworkers who try to help you feel better fast. Family members are often the most persistent in trying to help their loved ones get fixed. Perhaps it's just a symptom of larger problems in our society, which demands quick fixes for just about everything. No one wants to deal with loss and sadness for an extended period of time. "Bounce back," they tell us thoughtlessly. And when they do, they inadvertently cause the bereaved to feel guilty about their weeping and mood swings.

Season 3: Healing

John Dalton has come to believe that the third and final phase is a time of renewal, resurging energy, and, for the Christian, emotional healing. A nonreligious counselor might call this, says John, "healthy psychological adjustment." Motivation, ambition, creativity, and meaningful relationships gradually return.

Life becomes more normal again, but never the same. The events that once caused so much pain can be discussed with an emotional detachment and freedom that may even offend others who expect the deceased to be remembered with more feeling. Of course, some scars never heal. Some memories are never forgotten, but the searing pain and debilitating emotions become a thing of the past.

Blessed are those who mourn, **for they will be comforted.**

MATTHEW 5:4

> I will exalt you, O Lord,
> for you lifted me out of the depths
> and did not let my enemies gloat over me.
> O Lord my God, I called to you for help
> and you healed me.
> O Lord, you brought me up from the grave;
> you spared me from going down into the pit.
>
> Sing to the Lord, you saints of his;
> praise his holy name.
> For his anger lasts only a moment,
> but his favor lasts a lifetime;
> **weeping may remain for a night,**
> **but rejoicing comes in the morning.** PSALMS 30:1-5

Those who sow in tears
will reap with songs of joy.
He who goes out weeping,
carrying seed to sow,
will return with songs of joy. PSALMS 126:5-6

THE STAGES OF GRIEF

The seasons or "stages" of bereavement, then, are not entirely orderly and predictable, because everyone experiences grief differently. Dave Murrow, who lost his seventeen-year-old son Daniel in a drowning accident two years ago, wrote to me:

Grief is something you go through without an instruction manual. And no matter how many folks gather around you, ultimately it is something you must do alone.

My grandmother was nicknamed "Kitty." She was soft, gentle, and very wise. She died when I was a boy and never knew my son Daniel. But I know they would have loved each other!

Grandma Kitty lost a daughter, two sons, and her husband while she was still a young woman, and she was in the habit of saying, "Most of the learning is in the doing." She understood about those things.

You can't prepare for your child's death. You can't anticipate what it's going to be like. You can't even begin to get ready for something like that. When it comes, you just gotta do it—and learn.

Grief is a terribly lonely place, yet nearly everyone will experience certain aspects of the grief *process*. Nearly all the experts agree that grieving is unlike any other human experience, that you don't fully know what it's like until you've been there, and that just about everybody will experience at one time or another a full range of emotions: disbelief, denial, anger, depression, fear, guilt and forgiveness, the ability to cope, and the peace of resolution.

Grief Is . . .

The experience of grief is universal and felt by every person during the course of a lifetime.... Grief is an important, normal response to the loss of any significant object or person. It is an experience of deprivation and anxiety which can show itself physically, emotionally, cognitively, socially and spiritually. Any loss can bring about grief: divorce, retirement from one's job, amputations, death of a pet or plant, departure of a child to college or of a pastor to some other church, moving from a friendly neighborhood, selling one's car, losing a home or valued object, loss of a contest or athletic game, health failures, and even the loss of confidence or enthusiasm. Doubts, the loss of one's faith, the waning of one's spiritual vitality, or the inability to find meaning in life can all produce a sadness and emptiness which indicate grief. Indeed, whenever a part of life is removed there is grief.... *Most discussions of grief, however, concern losses which come when a loved one or other meaningful person has died.*

Gary Collins[5]

Early in this century, Sigmund Freud was one of the first to publish careful studies on grief. His purpose was to understand the process of mourning and the effort necessary to work through the grief, so he coined the now common term "grief work."

In 1944, a Harvard professor named Erich Lindemann wrote about his interviews with hundreds of grieving parents who had lost their children in the spectacularly tragic Coconut Grove fire, which claimed the lives of nearly five hundred young adults. In his study, Lindemann found that most people had four basic responses to the death of a loved one:

- Physical sensations
- An intense preoccupation with thoughts of the dead person
- Hostility and anger, usually marked by feelings of guilt
- Disturbances of the normal behavior patterns of the individual[6]

This whole process may go on for months, or even years. In *Help for Your Grief*, Arthur Freese notes that managing and overcoming the grief process involves three elements: getting yourself free from bondage to the one who died, readjusting to life without the deceased, and building new relationships. Success in the grief process also depends on "how well the mourner overcomes the human tendency to avoid the pain and distress of grief and the desire to evade the expression of the sufferer's true emotions."[7]

The principle challenge for those dealing with loss is to release their grief. This involves respecting, specifying, and expressing painful thoughts and feelings associated with the loss. To get beyond grief one must go through it, not around it. Nor are there any painless shortcuts.

JOHN A. LARSEN[8]

Other factors that influence a person's ability to work through grief include the individual's spiritual and emotional stability, the strength and support of personal relationships with others, the circumstances of the death, and the age of the person who died.[9] It's a fact that grief work when a child dies usually takes extra time and effort. One writer observes, "Most experts feel the loss of a child produces a permanent bereavement in the parents, particularly the mother."[10]

The simple idea that "time heals" is only partially true. Yes, it takes time, but you have to work on working out of your grief. It's not just going to go away. Grief doesn't "wear off in any simple manner, say, like a cold. A return to normality is a slow, complex, episodic process with many ups and downs. The grieving person can never be really sure just how he or she will be at any particular time or place."[11]

Grief even affects us physically, something a grieving person dare not ignore. In recent years, a number of studies have demonstrated the relationship between bereavement and physiological change. Physiological theory and research have found that loss may affect the immune system, lead to changes in the endocrine, autonomic nervous, and cardiovascular systems, and account for increased vulnerability to infection and disease.[12] In view of this, especially if you are in the early acute stage of grieving, it's important to let your doctor know what has happened in your life so he or she can monitor the indicators of your physical well-being.

GRIEF AND THE CHRISTIAN BELIEVER

The overwhelming effect of the death of a loved person lies in the very nature of the phenomenon of separation—probably the most basic and painful of all human experiences. Yet this is a situation every one of us must suffer through again and again during our lifetimes.

ARTHUR FREESE[13]

So don't pretend that you're OK when really you are dying inside. And don't think that just because you are a good Christian, it's not going to hurt as much. In fact, it might hurt more, because you may have thought God would not let something like this happen to you. But, as the apostle Paul declares, "You must not carry on over them like people who have nothing to look forward to, as if the grave were the last word. Since Jesus died and broke loose from the grave, God will most certainly bring back to life those who died in Jesus" (1 Thessalonians 4:13-14, *The Message*).

Paul is telling us here that grief is normal and painful, but for the Christian, it's not hopeless, because we believe we will be reunited with our loved ones in heaven. Moreover, our hope is not just that God will keep our loved ones alive or that he will never let them die. That's just not going to happen. You and I wish (not hope) otherwise, but death for everyone is a reality of life.

So you hope that nothing bad will ever happen. But even if the worst happens—if someone dies, if your child dies—it's not the end for the Christian. Our hope is not in tomorrow, it's in life after tomorrow; it's in the future that God promises to those who love and trust him.

"Do not let your hearts be troubled," Jesus said. "Trust in God; trust also in me. In my father's house are many rooms; if it were not so, I would have told you. I am going there to prepare a place for you. And if I go and prepare a place for you, I will come back and take you to be with me that you also may be where I am" (John 14:1-3).

Yes, grief is real for everyone. There are no exceptions. Everyone will experience different aspects of the grief process, although never in the same sequence or with the same intensity each step along the way. The next few chapters are about some of the most common feelings and experiences of grief work: disbelief and denial; anger and depression; panic, anxiety, and fear; guilt and forgiveness; and memories. Read and be healed.

THREE

I Can't Believe It!
Shock, Disbelief, and Denial

How could things go on when the world has come to an end? How could I go on in this void? How could one person, not very big, leave and emptiness that was galaxy-wide?

SHELDON VANAUKEN

It's a rainy, windy night as I begin to write this chapter. Just a moment ago I leaned over my desk to slide the window closed. Raindrops were blowing in on my Bible. Through the little crack I left open, I can hear distant thunder.

Not too far to the north, an ambulance is crying in the wet darkness. And after a few moments, another. And now I hear a third.

Somewhere tonight, not far from my home, right now, some nameless souls have had something terrible happen to them. And as the telephone calls fill the night, friends and family will listen, stunned. "I can't believe it," they are sure to say.

FOR WHOM THE BELL TOLLS

I think a lot about those folks when I hear the howl of an emergency vehicle. Perhaps I'm just melancholy. Or maybe it's because I'm a pastor and I've seen so much suffering firsthand and have had so many ask me for answers to unanswerable questions. I guess that's why, when I hear a distant siren, I think to myself, *I wonder if that's for someone in our congregation?*

Just yesterday, a mother and her daughter, Christi, were in a serious auto crash. We've known them well for years. Our daughters grew up together. When I called their home, Christi answered the phone. She had been driving the car at the time of the accident, she told me. Fortunately, her injuries were minor.

I spoke to her for less than two minutes and then called her dad to the phone, but can you guess what she said to me in those brief moments? I wrote it down, word for word: "It was pretty crazy. You don't think it can happen to you." Disbelief. She couldn't believe it happened, although right now she's trying harder than ever to believe in God and his healing presence.

> They will come and shout for joy
> on the heights of Zion;
> they will rejoice in the bounty of
> the Lord—
> the grain, the new wine and the oil,
> the young of the flocks and the herds.

They will be like a well-watered garden,
and they will sorrow no more.
Then maidens will dance and be glad,
young men and old as well.
I will turn their mourning into gladness;
I will give them comfort and joy
instead of sorrow. JEREMIAH 31:12-13

Then I saw a new heaven and a new earth, for the first heaven and the first earth had passed away.... And I heard a loud voice from the throne saying, "Now the dwelling of God is with men, and he will live with them. They will be his people, and God himself will be with them and be their God. **He will wipe every tear from their eyes. There will be no more death or mourning or crying or pain, for the old order of things has passed away."** REVELATION 21:1-4

It's raining again. Hard. The sound of the sirens has gone silent. Dutifully notified of the accident, friends and family are probably silent, too. They can't believe it happened. Right now, tonight, friends and relatives are experiencing an unfeeling cold and empty numbness. And tomorrow when they get up to face the new day, tonight will seem like a dream—a bad dream—and they'll say it again and again: "I can't believe it."

"I can't believe she's gone." I couldn't tell you how many times my wife, Marilyn, and I have said this since her mother's sudden death just a few years ago. I have twenty years of tender memories of our family—Marilyn and me and our three children—vacationing at Grandpa and Grandma's tiny, lovely citrus and avocado farm in southern California.

Visits there since her death have not been the same. I can feel her presence, and even more, her absence. When I look at family pictures, I think I stare at my mother-in-law's face the longest. She's gone. And still I can't believe it.

This is everyone's fear and eventually everyone's reality.

Shock. Speechless disbelief. In his classic work *A Severe Mercy*,

Sheldon Vanauken wrote of his wife, "The loss of Davy, after the intense sharing and closeness of the years, the loss and grief was, quite simply, the most immense thing I had ever known."[1]

Dave Murrow, whose teenage son drowned two years ago, wrote to me:

It has been seventeen months, and there's a part of me that is still not sure what happened. I go to Daniel's grave. I look at the pictures from the hospital, photos of him in a coma, struggling to return to this life.

And some rational part of me says, "Oh, yes, I remember. He died." But then another part of me says, I don't believe that. It couldn't be true. Not Dan. Not me. Not us. Not *my* son. Not *my* God. Not *my* life in such disarray.

Yet I was there. I lived each moment. Saw it all take place. I turned off the life support. I held his hand and cradled his head as he breathed his last breath.

I spoke at his funeral. I know that it is true, but somehow it's not. I know it to be a fact, but somehow it seems like some terrible fiction.

<hr>

The Initial Reaction—Those First Few Days

This is a period which no mourner can describe clearly, thanks to Nature's protective measures. Afterward, looking back, it is recalled as through a rolling mist which thins out occasionally to permit short glimpses of a distant blurred landscape, partly in sun and partly in blackest shadows.... Possibly the key word here is *shock*....

The initial response on hearing the news or seeing it actually happen is invariably one of numb disbelief: "I don't believe it." When a call told me a very dear friend had died in a matter of minutes from a sudden heart attack, I gave an anguished, "Oh—no... it can't be." And as I write this less than three years later, the anguish still floods back—the tears, the terrible emptiness and the pain. As Dr. Volkan commented to me in our discussion not long after this friend had died: "Your friend will always live inside of you," and he was right....

Mercifully, Nature covers the bereaved with a protective emotional blanket within minutes of the death news—there is a cold, empty numbness, a confused, dazed feeling of unreality that takes over....

Survivors often wonder that they "have no feelings" when the death occurs; actually this is the normal numbness that moves so fast they're not even aware of the first reaction.

ARTHUR FREESE[2]

UNPREPARED FOR WENDY'S DEATH

You need to know that your shock, disbelief, and numbness are absolutely normal responses to your loss. Margie Dalton, who has lost four children, wrote to me:

I was totally unprepared for Wendy's death. I was frightened and wanted to run away from it. Funeral arrangements? Why, I had never been to a funeral in my life! What should we do? My legalistic religious training had taught me to smile, to say that it must be God's will, and above all—for the sake of our "testimony" (it was more like our Christian facade)—to show that I was coping, to put on a show of strength.

But inside I was seething with anger. I was angry with God for allowing this to happen. I was angry at the doctors for not doing something more. I was just plain angry, but didn't know what to do with it.

Shock lessens the pain. I am convinced we lose brain cells in times of intense shock.[3] Life became a daze for me, and things would get done only because, like a robot, I would do the same things I had done for years—cleaning, washing, cooking. But it was all without emotion, without meaning.

When I think back now, I laugh at the number of times we ate macaroni and cheese. I would go grocery shopping and forget where I had parked the car. People's names would escape my memory. And reading! I would sometimes have to reread a paragraph as many as five times before I would remember what I had just read.

And Judy Hawk, who speaks and counsels on grief out of her personal experience of loss, wrote:

During the week following our son Robert's death, my husband, Lyle, and I found ourselves functioning quite well! It wasn't until weeks later that we realized what a blessing God gives with shock. We were able to meet and talk with other people in a normal way. We could even talk about our son Robert—and share our very personal stories of his life—without breaking down.

During the visitation, when his body was lying in the mortuary, hundreds of people filed by and many wept. But we kept our composure, talked openly of Robert's life, and even laughed!

The day of Robert's funeral, more than one thousand people attended. Robert, you see, was a police officer who had been killed in the line of duty. We will never forget the procession after the service, where hundreds of officers and other public officials participated in a grand parade of support.

Later, though, as the numbing shock of our loss wore off, grief and loneliness gripped our lives. Little did we realize at the time how much the love and support we received shortly after Robert's death would sustain us in the weeks and months ahead.

Writing of the death of his wife, an event immortalized by the motion picture *Shadowlands*, C. S. Lewis confessed a mental and emotional confusion not unlike Margie Dalton's:

No one told me that grief felt so like fear. I am not afraid, but the sensation is like being afraid. The same fluttering in the stomach, the same restlessness, the yawning. I keep on swallowing.

At other times it feels like being mildly drunk, or concussed. There is a sort of invisible blanket between the world and me. I find it hard to take in what anyone says. Or perhaps, hard to want to take it in. It is so uninteresting. Yet I want the others about me. I dread the moments when the house is empty. If only they would talk to one another and not to me.[4]

C. S. LEWIS[4]

You are in shock.
Nothing seems real.
You are not there.
People talk to you,
you do not respond....

These are signs of a temporary
paralysis that acts as a
protective mechanism.

EARL A. GROLLMAN[5]

TRUSTING GOD WHEN IT HURTS

Ben Applegate served for many years as the captain of the *Anastasis*, a huge ship and humanitarian outreach ministry of Youth With A Mission (YWAM). I had the joy of spending a week with Ben and his wife Helen a few years ago, when she gave me a copy of her new book *Anchor in the Storm*. They lost two daughters: one to meningitis, the other a few years later in a bizarre accident.

While serving as a missionary in Egypt, their oldest daughter, Susan, cut her finger on the edge of a tin can of beef. The resulting infection took her life in a few short days. Helen remembers her anguish in a chapter simply titled "Oh, No!"

I pushed the door open with both arms full of groceries. I could not wait to put them down, get lunch ready, and finally relax a bit. It was exactly seven weeks since I'd heard Susan's voice over the crackle of that overseas call. I certainly did miss her, but was glad now to have a few minutes of solitude while my other two girls were at school. As I headed toward the kitchen table, I almost dove into Ben, standing in my way.

"Whatever are you doing home at this time of the morning?" I asked, perplexed.

Ben looked at me strangely.

"What's happened, Ben? What's the matter?"

"You had better put your things down and come in the other room. I've got some bad news to tell you."

He walked me into the lounge and we sat down on our tweed sofa. What could be so wrong?

"Helen, I got a call from our pastor. Don Stephens [the Director of YWAM Mercy Ships] called him from Europe to get in touch with us."

….Ben lowered his eyes and continued, "There's a girl who died six days ago in Egypt by the name of Susan Applegate."

Listen to Helen's response:

Disbelief and denial flooded my mind. "Oh, that's silly," I retorted. "They've got the names mixed up." Why, we had just received a letter from Susan yesterday. She had spent a day at the beach and sounded as healthy and happy as ever…."No, it couldn't be our Susan," I repeated, trying to reassure myself and Ben.

"Well, we had better send a telex… to find out for sure," Ben responded. Quietly, he turned and headed for the kitchen phone.

The minutes ticked by on our large clock on the mantel while I waited in the lounge, motionless. As I heard Ben's voice from the kitchen, talking to the telex operator, I began to absorb the possibility that this terrible news really could be true. A band tightened around my chest. Maybe it wasn't just a silly mistake.

Maybe it was Susan! Maybe something horrible had happened. Maybe she really had died.

I started crying as I began to argue with my feelings. *No, it's not true! She's as healthy as a horse. No, it couldn't be!* I shouted silently to myself.

As the next few minutes passed, however, a grim certainty gripped me. I looked up despairingly, gazing out our large glass window and out onto the empty road. "Lord," I said, broken, "You've done it again. You've taken one of my children."

I sat there, my shoulders stooped over as I continued staring out at the empty road and reviewed our life. First, Jenny's brain damage, the long struggle, then defeat as we buried her.... Now this.

And here's the big question:

Once again, I was faced with a choice. Could I let go and accept the possible loss of another daughter? *Could I still trust a God who might permit another such terrible blow?*

In my numb state, I struggled as I fought to lay aside this growing certainty. Finally, I said to the Lord, "If this is true, You must have a very good reason for taking her." Slowly, that same peace I had first experienced when I'd prayed concerning Susan's marriage enveloped me as I made myself offer up my daughter to Him. "I give Susan willingly," I stammered, "because I know it's better for her to be with You."[6]

For three agonizing days Ben and Helen waited for the telex that finally confirmed Susan's death. Another three days passed, and a letter from her friend in Egypt arrived:

After a blood test was taken, Susan was given a transfusion and five pints of blood. At 8:00 P.M. that night, she seemed to be feeling great and wanted to go home. I insisted that she stay since more tests needed to be taken. Then, suddenly, as I stood next to her bed, her face almost seemed aglow as she exclaimed, "Monir, that music! Listen to that lovely music! It's as though I'm in a big cathedral and there's a beautiful choir!"

After gently explaining to Susan that I couldn't hear anything, she begged me to get the nurse, who was a friend of hers, certain that she would hear the music.

As I hurried to the door to find the nurse, I panicked as a new and fearful thought seized me. Whirling around, I raced back to Susan but it was too late. The heavenly host, their voices raised in song, had already taken her home.[7]

Hear my prayer, O Lord;
let my cry for help come to you.
Do not hide your face from me
when I am in distress.
Turn your ear to me;
when I call, answer me quickly.

For my days vanish like smoke;
my bones burn like glowing embers.
My heart is blighted and withered like grass;
I forget to eat my food.
Because of my loud groaning
I am reduced to skin and bones....

For I eat ashes as my food
and mingle my drink with tears
because of your great wrath,
for you have taken me up
and thrown me aside.
My days are like the evening shadow;
I wither away like grass.

But you, O Lord, sit enthroned forever;
your renown endures through all generations.
You will arise and have compassion on Zion....

For the Lord will rebuild Zion
and appear in his glory.
He will respond to the prayer of the destitute;
he will not despise their plea. PSALMS 102:1-17

Why Are You So Afraid?
The Fear of Death and
All the Fears Death Brings

> He is torn from the security of his tent and
> marched off to the king of terrors.
>
> JOB 18:14

I've stood at the head end of numberless open caskets. It's the proper thing for a pastor to do at the conclusion of the funeral. As family and friends file by to pay their last respects, I find it fascinating to study their faces.

A few pause fearlessly in front of the casket and stare into the gray face of the deceased. Even fewer reach down to touch the body. Most people rush by as quickly as they can, trying their very best not to appear hurried.

Many, perhaps half or more, refuse to even glance at the dead person. And strangely, most prefer not to make eye contact with me. Was it my sermon? Or is it because somehow, at that moment, I'm standing in for God?

Every death is a moment of truth for those who know the person who died. Dead. Indeed, the very word is unpleasant, as in "He's *dead*."

"Necrophobia," the pathological fear of death, is a fear that stifles ambition and can smother spouse and children through overprotectiveness. It was this sort of intense fear that the writer to the Hebrews addressed when he told how Christ, through his death on the cross, broke the power of the devil to "free those who all their lives were held in slavery by their fear of death" (Hebrews 2:15). The man or woman without Christ can become a slave to fear.

Billy Graham[1]

The Fear of Death

Why is death so frightful? Because, whether or not we like to admit it, death is the focal point and climax of everything that's wrong with the human race. It's about sorrow and loss, about saying good-bye—maybe forever. It's about accidents and disease, hurricanes and earthquakes. It's about murder, capital punishment, and abortion. It's about holding human beings hostage. It's about war.

It's about what the whole world is coming to. *It's about the consequences of humankind's rebellion against God and his Word.*

Death is so dreadful that most of the time we deny it. We even deny that we deny it! Oh, sure, we know everybody's going to die. I know it, too. But I really don't think much about it happening to me. I once had a seminary professor who startled our class by announcing, "When my wife and I had our four children, we opened up four more graves." People are born to die, but we keep having children without a second thought about them *ever* dying.

Think about it. We are in so much denial over death that when someone we know is dying, we hardly know what to say, so we reassure them that everything is going to be OK. I have no research to back this up, but I suspect that nearly every terminal cancer patient has had at least one person tell them, "It's going to be all right!" Or, "You're going to make it!" What in the world do we mean by that?

Now, I know what some of you may be thinking: What about the healing power of God? What about research that shows a positive attitude, even apart from religious faith, can put cancer into remission? *I am not even slightly suggesting that we shouldn't pray for healing, or that we shouldn't hope against hope for the very best.*

Yet the very fact that we hope and pray is everyone's unconscious admission that death should not happen to human beings, that something inside us is supposed to live forever. The Bible is quite clear on this. God did not, in fact, create us to die. That came later, when the first people fell into sin. And ever since then, we've been fugitives from the penalty—fearing death, running from death, denying death.

The conversation at the party became hushed as someone reported that a friend had just been told he had incurable cancer. A psychiatrist—a strong, handsome man who was a prominent member of the social and professional community—said, "I'm scared to death of dying." He smiled sheepishly at his feeble pun, but he had honestly expressed what so many people feel.

In spite of rapid and ever-increasing advances in medical technology and pain relief, no one has found a way to lessen people's fear of dying. This is not some new psychosis but a condition as old as man. David, the bold youth who defied the giant Goliath, is the same man who cried out, "My heart is in anguish within me; the terrors of death assail me. Fear and trembling have beset me; horror has overwhelmed me" (Psalms 55:4, 5).

Age and circumstance often dictate the degree of fear a person may feel with facing death. David did not say those words when he was a teenager facing Goliath, but when he was older and had experienced sickness and betrayal by friends. Sometimes the fear of death grows significantly with age.

Jesus' disciples were rugged men, physically toughened by living outdoors and traveling long distances on foot. And yet when they were caught in a sudden storm so common in the area of Galilee, they shouted desperate fear, "Lord, save us! We are going to drown!" (Matthew 8:25). They were terrified that they were going to die.

My friend, Jack Black, has defined fear as "an emotion that speaks of dread, fright, alarm, panic, trepidation, and consternation." All human beings capable of thinking manifest these emotions. Thus, fear is universal in all times and places. It is a normal, human response to the unknown. And death, the experience of death, is an unknown.

BILLY GRAHAM[2]

Fear of death, then, is perfectly normal. As strange as it may seem, it's part of God's plan. Not his best plan, mind you, but his plan, nevertheless. The Bible doesn't take very long to get around to this point. In the third chapter of the first book, Genesis (only the third page in my Bible), God warns, "You must not eat fruit from the tree that is in the middle of the garden, and you must not touch it, or *you will die*" (Genesis 3:3). And when Adam and Eve did just that, God swore:

By the sweat of your brow
you will eat your food
until you return to the ground,
since from it you were taken;
for dust you are
and to dust you will return. GENESIS 3:19

If you say you have no fear of death, you are either in denial or you are the rarest of human beings. And if it's true that you don't fear your own death, what about the death of the ones you love most? Do you fear that?

The fear of death is natural and is present in everyone, [and] it is the basic fear that influences all others, a fear from which no one is immune, no matter how disguised it may be. William James spoke very early for this school, and with his usual colorful realism he called death "the worm at the core" of many pretensions to happiness.

ERNEST BECKER[3]

The Bible is also quite clear on God's only solution to the sin and death problem. His only answer is his only Son. The fear of death is as much a part of human life as death itself, and this is part of God's plan to urge us to humble ourselves before him and invite the Lord Jesus into our hearts. Jesus said, "I am the resurrection and the life. He who believes in me will live, even though he dies; and whoever lives and believes in me will never die. Do you believe this?"[4] There really is no alternative.

The Bible also teaches that people fear dying because after death comes the judgment. Every person must stand before God and give an account of his or her life, which brings us right back to Jesus. No one's efforts to be religious or to be good are good enough. Everyone falls short of the glory of God.

To put it in more contemporary terms, everyone's relationship with God is thoroughly dysfunctional, without a sliver of hope of fixing it on our own. There is no one who is good in God's sight. No, not one.[5] Except his Son. "Salvation is found in no one else," the Bible tells us, "for there is no other name under heaven given to men by which we must be saved" (Acts 4:12). Jesus himself said, "I am the way and the truth and the life. No one comes to the Father except through me" (John 14:6).

The death of a loved one unleashes a legion of wild fears, but I am convinced that all have their roots in the primal fear, the fear of death itself—and what's beyond death: the judgment throne of God. So if you are full of fears, your first step toward healing, if you have not already done this, is to make peace with God by asking Jesus into your heart. And even if you have already done that, you may want to relive the moment by inviting Jesus back to be Lord of your life.

You can pray this prayer right now:

Dear Lord Jesus, I believe you died on the cross for my sin. I also believe that you were raised from the dead to give me the assurance that there is life after death. Right now I invite you to come into my life and be my Savior and Lord. I feel utterly helpless in the face of my loss, and I desperately need you to work in my life. I believe in you, but I am praying to you now because I need the reassurance of your love for me. And I really need to know that when I die, I'm going to heaven. Thank you for hearing me and coming into my heart. In Jesus' name, Amen.

The Fears that Death Brings

"What's going to happen
to me?"

Your muscles are tight and
tense.
Your mind races.
You cannot think clearly.
Simple routine decisions
become major problems.

You are emotionally disorganized:

alone,
confused,
helpless,
hopeless.

EARL A. GROLLMAN[6]

The fear of death is the root of all fears, so when someone dies, many other fears in your life will surface. There's so much to worry about. We live in what has been called "the age of anxiety," and that's when everything is "normal." Add to the mix a major trauma, or the death of a loved one, and your fears can become downright paralyzing.

Fears

When a loved one has died, your life will be altered, perhaps even shattered. Normal routines are no longer normal, and new routines have to be developed. Roles within your family may have to be redefined. You may be on shaky ground, feeling very unsure of yourself and unsure of your future. It is during this period that you may become fearful of things you used to be comfortable with. You may jump at loud noises; you may be afraid to go out alone, fearful of new situations, afraid that someone else will die, afraid of driving down busy highways, afraid of the dark, or perhaps afraid of the particular room in your home in which your loved one died.

HELEN FITZGERALD[7]

The Bible uses the words *fear, worry,* and *anxiety* interchangeably to describe the same basic human emotion. The New Testament Greek word for anxiety means, simply, "to be distracted," or "to take responsibility for someone or something." Christian psychologist and author Gary Collins calls this "realistic concern" and reassures us that "according to the Bible, there is nothing wrong with realistically acknowledging and trying to deal with the identifiable problems of life. To ignore danger is foolish and wrong. But it is also wrong, as well as unhealthy, to be immobilized by excessive worry."[8]

And there's nothing like death to bring on "excessive worry," so it's to your benefit if you learn how to work through your fears. Facing your fears and working through them are necessary steps in the grief process.

But how? What does the Bible teach us about managing and overcoming our fears? I think 2 Timothy 1:7 is key: "For God has not given us the spirit of fear, but of *power*, and of *love*, and of a *sound mind*" (KJV). Three wonderful words, and three principles to keep your fears from holding you hostage: *power*, *love*, and a *sound mind*.

THE POWER OF GOD'S PERSONAL PRESENCE

Ultimately, the only way a person can overcome fear is by the power of the presence of God, because like everything else in life, fear is fundamentally a spiritual issue. This is why the Bible repeatedly implores us, "*Fear not!*" In fact, it says "fear not" over three hundred times!

But now, this is what the Lord says—
he who created you, O Jacob,
he who formed you, O Israel:
"**Fear not**, for I have redeemed you;
I have called you by name;
you are mine.
When you pass through the waters,
I will be with you;
and when you pass through the rivers,
they will not sweep over you.
When you walk through the fire,
you will not be burned;
the flames will not set you ablaze.
For I am the Lord, your God,
the Holy One of Israel, your Savior." ISAIAH 43:1-3

So healing from your fear starts with faith. Even scientific research has upheld the power of faith to overcome fear. Studies of military personnel in combat situations have demonstrated that belief in God is a principal factor in overcoming fear.[9] Jesus said, "Therefore I tell you [he feels strongly about this!], *do not worry about your life....* Look at the birds of the air; they do not sow or reap or store away in barns, and yet your heavenly Father feeds them. Are you not much more valuable than they? Who of you by worrying can add a single hour to his life?" [Emphasis added]

"See how the lilies of the field grow," he adds. "They do not labor or spin. Yet I tell you [he feels strongly about this too!] that not even Solomon in all his splendor was dressed like one of these. If that is how God clothes the grass of the field, which is here today and tomorrow is thrown into the fire, will he not much more clothe you, O you of little faith?" (Matthew 6:25-30).

O you of little faith! Now, don't take this wrong. There's so much shaming that goes on in Christian circles that it would be easy to get the idea that Jesus is down on you, too. Jesus isn't scolding you for not trusting more in God. And you don't need to be told something you already know, that your faith probably isn't what it should be.

Actually, Jesus is trying to help you see things from heaven's point of view. To remind you how much the heavenly Father really does care about you. To help you break out of the grip of your fear. In fact, Jesus could not be more tender. Think about it. Jesus is helping you understand the mystery of the Father's provision in terms of flowers and little birds. Death is an ugly intrusion into the profusion of life around us.

Take a moment right now. Step outside your home. Or if the weather is unpleasant, look out the window. Look at the trees, the sky. Is it springtime? Look especially at the grass, the flowers, the birds. You are surrounded by a world of living messages of God's loving provision. "O you of little faith. Who of you by worrying can add a single hour to his life?"

Anxiety is unbelief in disguise.

DON HAWKINS

Worry is not only foolish, but also God-less, because it slanders God's care for men.

COLIN BROWN

There is nothing that wastes the body like worry, and one who has any faith in God should be ashamed to worry about anything whatsoever.

MAHATMA GANDHI

Cast all your anxiety on him because he cares for you.

1 PETER 5:7

NO FEAR OF THE FUTURE

Overcoming your fear starts with faith in God and trust in his plan for your future. Realistically, the future is uncertain. Sometimes we hear people say, "You have to have hope." But hope in what? The future? As though the future has some power of its own?! Apart from a relationship with God, hoping is more like groping. The future is nothing but a dream without the confidence that somehow God holds the future.

When Martin Luther King, Jr. looked to the future and proclaimed his now immortal words, "I have a dream," he spoke not of an anchorless possibility but of a certain hope. King's hope, often lost in the rhetoric of social reform, was grounded in his faith in God, not just in a noble sense of justice and civil rights. In other words, without God, dreams are illusions and hope is hopeless.

Fear is about the uncertainties of tomorrow. Faith is confidence that the God of eternity has already been where you're going and that he's going to take care of you when you get there. You don't always know how, but you know him. To say it another way, God has a plan for your ultimate future that supersedes your immediate future.

No matter what happens tomorrow or the next day, there will always be another day, even after the day you die. Jesus said to the thief on the cross, "Today you will be with me in paradise." God's future is always one day ahead of your worst day. Death never has the last word. God does.

Do not let your hearts be troubled. Trust in God; trust also in me. In my Father's house are many rooms; if it were not so, I would have told you. I am going there to prepare a place for you.

JOHN 14:1-2

Do you see it all come together in this verse? Fear and faith are incompatible. And faith is fixed on the certain future of God's plan. Overcoming fear starts with faith. Faith in God. Faith in God's future. You may fear today, but the promises of God are waiting for you tomorrow, and those promises are made real by the abiding presence of God's Holy Spirit.

> The Counselor, the Holy Spirit, whom the Father will send in my name, will teach you all things and will remind you of everything I have said to you. Peace I leave with you; my peace I give you. I do not give to you as the world gives. Do not let your hearts be troubled and do not be afraid. JOHN 14:26-27

Jesus promises two things in this passage: to send the Spirit and to leave us his peace. In the subtle parallelism of this verse, it's almost as though Jesus is giving the Holy Spirit a name: "Peace." The Holy Spirit is the wonderful Counselor, the bearer of God's presence and peace. Dale Simpson, who is the Clinical Director of Family Life Counseling Services, writes that "the Holy Spirit must work into believers God's peace. This peace results from a relationship with him and not simply from positive thinking or some other cognitive technique."[10]

Ultimately, then, the only way a person can overcome fear is by the power of the presence of God. "God has not given us the spirit of fear; but of *power.*"

THE POWER OF LOVE

Love is another life-giving principle to keep your fears from holding you hostage. Let's talk about how this works. First of all, fear and anxiety are rooted in self-needs. Now, there's nothing wrong with needing things. In fact, if you read the first few chapters of the Bible carefully, you'll discover that Adam had needs *before* he sinned: "The Lord God said, 'It is not good for the man to be alone. I will make a helper suitable for him'" (Genesis 2:18).

Needs are natural. To have self-needs is to be fully human in the way God originally created us. Being needy is not a result of Adam and Eve's disobedience and sin, but what has changed since the Fall is how we try to meet those needs *selfishly.* When your spiritual, mental, and emotional energies are invested in what *you* need, what *you* want, or what *you* think you need or want, you'll be anxious, troubled, and fearful. *This is love in the wrong direction.* Love in the wrong direction is self-serving.

Jesus addressed this in John 12:24-25: "I tell you the truth, unless a kernel of wheat falls to the ground and dies, it remains only a single seed. But if it dies, it produces many seeds." He's not talking about gardening! Anticipating his own fruitful death, Jesus is really discussing human nature and illustrating the difference between love in the wrong direction and love in the right direction.

"The man," he explains, "who loves his life [love in the wrong direction] will lose it, while the man who hates his life in this world will keep it for eternal life [love in the right direction]."

This is a tough verse, and it's easy to miss the point, especially if you've heard a lot of stuff about self-esteem, which really isn't the issue here. Or if you're in the middle of your grief and anguish, and you just can't stop thinking about yourself, and you feel guilty about that too. Well, that really is what Jesus is saying, but not unkindly. The more our mental and emotional energy is self-serving, the more miserable we'll be.

In other words, your pain in your loss may be immeasurable, but feeling sorry for yourself is probably the worst thing you can do. It's kind of like letting your pain and loss become your god. It's not selfish to feel pain, but it's self-defeating to let your pain and fear rule your life.

Selfishness is love turned outside in, but healing comes to us when we begin to turn our love inside out. And we can't just make this happen with a little extra willpower. I can't freely and fully love others unless I love God first, and I can't love God unless he loves me first! *Love that's moving in the right direction starts by moving from God to me.*

The apostle John wrote, "If anyone acknowledges that Jesus is the Son of God, God lives in him and he in God. And so we know and rely on the love God has for us. God is love. Whoever lives in love lives in God, and God in him…. *There is no fear in love. But perfect love drives out fear*" (1 John 4:15-18, emphasis added).

"We know and rely on the love God has for us." In other words, I can't fully love until I've received and experienced God's perfect love. My love is imperfect. Self-serving. God's love is unchanging. *Immutable* is the theological term. Unlike human emotional energy, something we like to call love, God's love *never* wavers. Therefore, God's love is perfect, or as the original Greek term in this verse means, "complete." "Perfect love" is the beginning and end of all love.

This perfect love of God liberates me from fear. My anxieties are lost in the perfect love of God. If God is for me, who can be against me?! Why should I have to worry about anything? God is on my side! Totally, completely, perfectly, and forever! *Only a relationship with God, nothing else, can ultimately liberate me from the prison of my fears.*

When we're in pain, we really can't help ourselves, and we find ourselves reaching out to God for the comfort and healing of his loving presence. Remember the vivid images of the Oklahoma City bombing? And remember our nation's response? President and Mrs. Clinton and Billy Graham shared the same platform in a huge memorial service in the heartland of America.

Tens of millions watched on television and wept with the families who lost their fathers and mothers, brothers and sisters, and children. And we all prayed. Even people who are not particularly religious probably prayed. Why? Because *only a relationship with God, nothing else, can ultimately liberate us from the prison of fear.* "Perfect love drives out fear."

I think this is why the Lord's Table is profoundly meaningful to Christians. Really, if you stop to analyze it as an outsider, the sacrament is silly. Eating a morsel of bread. Drinking a sip of grape juice or wine. But if you're a believer, the personal presence of God in that moment can be overwhelming. Theologians have debated the finer points of the Eucharist, and entire Christian movements have been defined by their doctrine of the bread and the wine and the body of Christ. Yet, for the person in the pew, what matters is that he or she is touching God and receiving his forgiveness and healing.

No matter where I personally "take Communion," I sense God's presence. It can happen to me anytime. As I remember what Jesus did for me, forgiveness and love wash over my soul in wondrous mystery. It's the unmerited grace and love of God coming to me in my moment of openness and faith.

So love that's moving in the right direction moves from God to me, but it doesn't stop there. God's love never allows me to be self-serving. It flows through me to others.

Love has been called the greatest therapeutic force of all, but nowhere is this more true than in the reduction of fear and anxiety.... One writer has suggested that "the enemy of fear is love; the way to put off fear, then, is to put on love.... Love is self-giving; fear is self-protecting. Love moves toward others; fear shrinks away from them.... The more fear, the less love, the more love, the less fear.

GARY COLLINS[11]

Simply stated, a most excellent way to press through your fear is to find some way to help someone else. Only in giving is there receiving. India's great leader Jawaharlal Nehru once wrote, "Logic and cold reason are poor weapons to fight fear.... Only faith *and generosity* [love in the right direction] can overcome them."

"... AND A SOUND MIND"

"For God has not given us the spirit of fear, but of *power*, and of *love*, and of a *sound mind*" [emphasis added]. Ultimately, the only way a person can overcome fear is by the power of the presence of God, because in God's presence are peace and love. But there's one more thing. God has also given us "a sound mind." In the original language of the New Testament, this word meant "mental health," in contrast to the Greek word for *crazy*, or *insane*.

And grief still feels like fear. Perhaps, more strictly, like suspense. Or like waiting; just hanging about waiting for something to happen. It gives life a permanently provisional feeling. It doesn't seem worth starting anything. I can't settle down. I yawn, I fidget, I smoke too much. Up till this I always had too little time. Now there is nothing but time. Almost pure time, empty successiveness.

C. S. LEWIS[12]

Fear, the Bible tells us, "hath torment."[13] It's almost as though every fear has an element of insanity. At least that's the way you feel on the deep end of fear. Panic sets in, and it's as if you're losing your mind. But God has not given us the spirit of fear, but of mental health.

This, I believe, is the practical side to overcoming fear. I am comforted to know that God has not only offered me his healing presence; he has also given me a sound mind—the gift of common sense—to help me get on with life. National mourning, like the kind we experienced for the families of the Oklahoma City bombing victims, doesn't last forever. At some point, we have to tear ourselves away from the television images and get on with life. It may be in fits and starts, but somewhere along the path of grief, we have to return to the normal activities of daily living.

A COMMONSENSE APPROACH TO FEAR

Here is a plan for approaching your fear.

You need to tell yourself the truth.

There are wise ways to win over your worries. Many fears you are experiencing in your loss are rooted in false notions. Even when we have real fears, most of the outcomes and consequences we fear are unrealistic. I once heard it said that over 90 percent of everything we fear never happens.

Today is the tomorrow you worried about yesterday. Is today really as awful as you thought tomorrow would be yesterday?

JAMES BECK[14]

Face your fears head-on.
Think about it. Fear teaches us to avoid unpleasant situations. This avoidance reduces our anxiety and rewards passivity, which in turn reinforces and strengthens our avoidance of the fear. Our futile attempts to resolve our fears by avoiding them actually become the means of perpetuating the fear!

Courage consists not in the absence of fear and anxiety, but of the capacity to move ahead, even though one is afraid. [In order to overcome fear, it is necessary] to move *through* the anxiety producing situations rather than moving *around* them or *retrenching* before them.

GARY COLLINS[15]

Panic

When a person begins worrying about losing his mind, he often panics. He becomes almost paralyzed with fear. It is often fear of the unknown, or fear of something he does not understand, that throws him into this panic.

It is important that we understand something about the grief process in advance of the crisis, so that we may eliminate the panic that accompanies fear of the unknown. When we have been briefed about some of the tricks which grief plays on our minds, then we are not overwhelmed by the disturbing thoughts that seek to take over. It is the panic of thinking we are going through something wholly abnormal that throws us deeper into despair. But it is not abnormal, it is normal! It is comforting to know that even panic is normal.

To help ourselves through such a period when we can think of nothing but our loss, we must be open to new and different human relationships. At a time like this all we want to do is run away from life. The last thing we care to do is try anything new. We can think of a hundred different reasons why we prefer to stay home and be gloomy rather than go out and be forced to be nice to people and think new thoughts. Such an attitude is natural; it is to be expected. We must not, however, allow in our gloom, for it will only prolong our grief work. And to work through grief is very hard work!

GRANGER E. WESTBERG[16]

Read and meditate on Philippians 4:4-10 at least once a day—and do what it says!

The Bible tells us, "Don't be anxious about anything." Unfortunately, you can't just stop being fearful by telling yourself, "I'm not going to worry about that." One Christian counselor and writer observed, "It is practically impossible to simply stop worrying. Such deliberate effort directs our attention to the problem and can increase anxiety rather than decrease it. A better approach is to focus on activities and thoughts which *indirectly* reduce anxiety."[17]

Here's a short list of things that will help calm your stress and depression so that you will be able to work through your fear.

- Sit outside and watch the sunrise or the sunset.

- Take a walk in the park.

- Relax in a comfortable chair. If you don't have one, get away to a nice hotel and relax by yourself in the lobby, or by the pool. I've visited numerous hotels in my area, for lunch or just to meet someone, without staying the night.

- Listen to soft music, like *Hosanna* worship tapes, available in your local Christian bookstore, or listen to light classical music.

Many composers of classical music were Christians! Take a portable cassette or CD player with headphones to the park or the nice hotel.

- Pet your dog or cat. A recent newspaper advertisement for a large medical center in my city indicated that, according to research, time with a pet can reduce stress.

- Exercise! Strenuous exercise has really helped me manage stress and depression in my personal life.

- Talk to a close friend about how you are feeling. And pray with him or her at least once a week.

- See a counselor or, perhaps, a physician. You may need medication to get you through the worst part of your fear.

- Don't put things off. Putting things off can cause more fear.

The Bible also has some advice for anxiety reduction. The verses that follow are from Philippians 4:4-10, *The Amplified Bible*.

Rejoice in the Lord
Rejoice in the Lord always—delight, gladden yourselves in Him; again I say, Rejoice! (4:4).

It's impossible to rejoice in your suffering. In your loss. In your pain and grief. But you can always rejoice in the Lord and his promises. And his provision in your life.

Be Kind to Others
Let all men know and perceive and recognize your unselfishness—your considerateness, your forbearing spirit. The Lord is near—He is coming soon (4:5).

In other words, let everyone see your kind, sweet, considerate, gracious attitude. When you are kind to others—love in the right direction—it refocuses your emotional energies away from your loss and anxiety. Perfect love casts out fear.

Talk to God about It

Do not fret or have any anxiety about anything, but in every circumstance and in everything by prayer and petition [definite requests] with thanksgiving continue to make your wants known to God. And God's peace [be yours, that tranquil state of soul assured of its salvation through Christ...] which transcends all understanding, shall garrison and mount guard over your hearts and minds in Christ Jesus (4:6-7).

What's the promise for talking to God about your fear? *Peace!* It's what you're looking for, right?

Think Positive!

Whatever is true, whatever is worthy of reverence and is honorable and seemly, whatever is just, whatever is pure, whatever is lovely and loveable, whatever is kind and winsome and gracious, if there is any virtue and excellence, if there is anything worthy of praise, think on and weigh and take into account these things—fix your minds on them (4:8).

God's Word is not specific here about what you should think about, and though Bible meditation is a necessary part of Christian growth, this verse does not limit positive thinking to just reflecting on the Bible. "*Whatever* is lovely" could refer to the sunset, or your cat.

Keep Doing the Right Thing

Practice what you have learned and received and heard and seen in me, and model your way of living on it, and the God of peace—of untroubled, undisturbed well-being—will be with you. (4:9).

What's the promise here for those who live right, even when they may have every reason not to? *Peace!* It's what you're looking for, isn't it?

Keep Loving in the Right Direction

I was made very happy in the Lord that now you have revived your interest in my welfare after so long a time; you were indeed thinking of me, but you had not opportunity to show it. (4:10)

Turn your love in the right direction! Help somebody else. And the God of peace will be with you! And his perfect love will drive away your fears.

The God of All Comfort

Over and over again God declares this: "I, even I, am he that comforteth you," He says to the poor, frightened children of Israel. And then He reproaches them with not being comforted. "Why," He says, "should you let anything make you afraid when here is the Lord, your Maker, ready and longing to comfort you. You have feared continually every day the 'fury of the oppressor,' and have forgotten Me..."

The God who exists is the God and Father of our Lord Jesus Christ, the God who so loved the world that He sent His son, not to judge the world, but to save it. He is the God who anointed the Lord Jesus Christ to bind up the brokenhearted, and to proclaim liberty to the captives, and the opening of the prison to them that are bound, and to comfort all that mourn. Please notice that *all*. Not a few selected ones only, but all. Every captive of sin, every prisoner in infirmity, every mourning heart throughout the whole world must be included in this "all." It would not be "all" if there should be a single one left out, no matter how insignificant, or unworthy, or even how feeble-minded that one might be.... Do not scold the feeble-minded, but comfort them. The very ones who need comfort most are the ones that our God, who is like a mother, wants to comfort—not the strong-minded ones, but the feeble-minded.

HANNAH WHITALL SMITH[18]

So You're Mad? At God?

Loneliness, Anger, and Depression

> *Look at my no-good neighbor.*
> *He's in perfect health!*
> *Why didn't he die?*
> *Why did this happen to my loved one,*
> *who was so wonderful?*
> *What kind of God would do this to me?*
> *It's all so unfair.*
>
> EARL A. GROLLMAN[1]

My wife Marilyn and I were spending a summer week in Salem, Oregon. The Pacific Northwest is a great place to visit in August, especially if you live in the Arizona desert.

I was teaching in a discipleship school for Youth With A Mission and I was just wrapping up the morning session when I heard our little son Matthew (he was probably five or six at the time) sobbing mournfully just outside the door of my classroom. He was looking for his mother, who was sitting in the back row.

After dismissing the students, I hurried outside to join my wife. "What's the matter?" I asked.

"Matthew had diarrhea," she answered with distress. "In his pants," she added.

It was a long walk up the hill to our guest room, and yes, Matthew cried the whole way. Between sobs, he whimpered something I'll never forget: "I asked Jesus to take the diarrhea away, and he didn't."

It was really a rather ordinary moment, but I was mad at God. After all, Jesus said, "If you have the faith of a little child, you can have just about anything you ask for." How does God expect me to believe in him for big things when he can't even hear my little boy in his misery?

I mean, what was I supposed to tell Matthew? "Son, if you prayed and read your Bible a little longer today, maybe you would not have gotten sick." Hardly! It's not very realistic to expect a five-year-old to understand the more subtle elements of healing faith.

So I said nothing. And God said nothing back.

Matthew's wailing subsided as his loving mom removed his soiled clothing and washed him clean of his filth. And his misery was forgotten in the bright, warm sunshine of an Oregon summer afternoon.

Silent Night

It is around noon on Christmas Eve. My beeper calls out the number for the Pediatric Intensive Care Unit. The nurse tells me an eight-year-old boy named John is being flown by helicopter to the hospital. He is in a diabetic coma, and his dad is flying in with him. *"Not on Christmas Eve,"* I say to myself, *"Not on Christmas Eve."*

I meet John's dad in the Pediatric Intensive Care waiting room. No one else is there. The hospital is quiet. It is Christmas Eve. He tells me John's mom is on the way in the car. He is very tearful as he waits to see his son. "I can't believe this is happening," he says over and over. The shock and disbelief are numbing.

I ask him to tell me what happened. As we sit, he tells me the story of the past few days many times. He starts in a different place each time, but he always ends with the same question—*"WHY?"* He wonders how all the symptoms of diabetes could have been missed, how he and John's mom just thought John was tired and needed more rest, how they had no idea he was this sick, and then, how he was finally rushed to the hospital. As he tells this, he breaks down and begins to cry. He beats his hands on the arms of the chair. I listen to him. I feel helpless.

He cries for a long time. We sit in the silence of his tears. There are no words now. Quietly, he says that he feels like he should have been able to do something different. He says he *should have known* that something was wrong with John. "Daddies are supposed to know," he screams. "Daddies are supposed to know." His guilt and helplessness are overwhelming. I think, *"Dear God, please not on Christmas Eve."*

John's mom arrives. Around 3:00 P.M. the doctors tell them John is brain dead. There is nothing more that can be done for him. Once more, we sit in silence as they hold each other while their tears flow and their hearts break.

…No one speaks. It seems that each person is lost in thought, maybe pondering in their hearts the mystery of life and death that is to be a part of this Christmas Eve.…

As John's mom and dad talk, they stroke his hair and caress his cheeks. In a whisper, John's dad begins to talk about Christmas. His voice drops. His tears fall. He tells of unopened presents under the tree, of special gifts and surprises. Haltingly, he tells of his hopes and dreams for John, and how he had tried to be a good daddy.

Finally, it is time to turn off the life support machines. The vigil is over. It is finished. His mom cries very hard, and then, gently, tenderly, softly, she bends down to her son. She kisses him on the forehead, and says, "I love you."

> *Silent Night, holy night,*
> *All is calm, all is bright*
> *Round yon Virgin Mother and child.*
> *Holy infant so tender and mild,*
> *Sleep in heavenly peace,*
> *Sleep in heavenly peace.*

With John's dad holding his hand, I say a prayer for him. My tears blind me. My heart chokes me. There are some words said about "for unto us a child is born, unto us a son is given."

With John's dad holding his hand, John's heart is stilled. There is peace on earth.

As I have remembered that night, somehow and some way, the time was holy. In the darkness, among the stories and the carols, the angels of heaven cried. On that cold night, we had no gifts to give. There was no gold or frankincense or myrrh, only the precious gift of each other. As we told our stories, we gave of our very selves, each to the other—maybe in unspeakable and sacred ways—but give we did.

In those long hours that were too short, in the laughter that was filled with tears, in the hope that was filled with fear, Christ was born and John died. A son is given.

Sleep in heavenly peace, little John, sleep in heavenly peace.

LOGAN JONES[2]

ANGRY? HOW ANGRY?

So how does this story make you feel? How does your own suffering and loss make you feel? Angry? How angry? Why? Why do people suffer and die? And why do they suffer and die in such untimely ways?

Wait a minute. *"Untimely* death?" Have you ever heard a more ridiculous expression? As though death is ever timely! As though there is ever a good time for suffering and pain! Margie Dalton, whom I introduced in an earlier chapter, wrote to me:

For a long period of time I wanted to know every detail of my son's climbing accident—every detail of every step the boys took that morning. It was very frustrating not to know. It made me very angry that these details were not available. Peter, the boy who had been with my son Tom on the day of his death, distanced himself from us and was discernibly unwilling and perhaps unable to share the events of that morning.

So I became increasingly bitter and hateful toward Peter. Several years after Tom's death (yes, it took me that long to deal with my anger), I finally had to seek Christian counsel and healing prayer for my bitterness. God in a wonderful way delivered me from the darkness of my hellish response and redeemed me from what could have been a lifelong prison of destructive thinking.

Bitterness and anger will kill the spirit within us, so we *must* let go. God will set us free when we come to Him for deliverance. It was only after I had passed through this time of forgiveness for my misdirected anger and healing from my offense that I was able to begin to see the larger picture of God's purposes in my loss. For the first time, I began to experience a renewed understanding of God's extravagant love, and I actually was given a vision of the hope of eternity.

HELPLESS IN THE SHADY VALLEY

Anger is often the result of our feelings of helplessness. If my lawn mower quits, or my car stalls, or my children disobey me, or the doctor tells me I have a heart condition that's not treatable, or my spouse has an affair, or my child dies, *I feel helpless.* And when I feel helpless, I get angry.

It is only in the valley of the shadow of death that I fully discover that the Lord is my shepherd. Most of the time I live as if my life will go on forever, uninterrupted by suffering and death, and in one sense, that's OK, because thinking about death is like looking directly into the sun. We can only handle so much of its intensity.

But death is as real as life, and sooner or later I must acknowledge its reality if I want to understand life. When I look into the face of death, I find myself asking the most important questions: Why do people die? and What's the purpose of living?

In the opening verses of Luke 13, some people challenged Jesus with these ultimate questions about the meaning of life and death:

Now there were some present at that time who told Jesus about the Galileans whose blood Pilate had mixed with their sacrifices.

Jesus answered, "Do you think that these Galileans were worse sinners than all the other Galileans because they suffered this way?

"I tell you [Are we listening?], **No! But unless you repent, you too will all perish."** LUKE 13:1-3

There are some great lessons here about the inappropriateness of Job-like moralizing, that is, trying to find a cause and effect in everything. (I will have more to say about this later.) But the most obvious thing we can learn from this scripture is that death, particularly sudden, unexpected, and unfair death, reminds us of the fragility of life. What matters most is whether or not we have a personal relationship with God.

Some years ago another pastor and I were attending a funeral. In the lobby of the church he leaned into my face and announced in a macabre sort of way, "I *love* to do funerals." "Love" was the longest word in the sentence, as in, "I *l-o-v-e* to do funerals."

Being fairly new to the ministry and having done only a couple of funerals myself, I stared at him in disbelief. "You *l-o-v-e* to do funerals?" I echoed.

"Yes," he replied, his voice full of deep conviction. "I love to do funerals because the needs are so profound and people are so open to God." Now I can say, years later, that I too l-o-v-e to do funerals, because of the unparalleled pastoral opportunities.

The deeper meaning of death is that it is a terrible reminder of human sin and failure and, concurrently, that we had better be in right relationship with God. In the face of death, we have the opportunity to discover eternal life and how to get it—through Christ.

On his arrival, Jesus found that Lazarus had already been in the tomb for four days....

"Lord," Martha said to Jesus, "if you had been here, my brother would not have died. [Lots of people have said this to God.] But I know that even now God will give you whatever you ask."

Jesus said to her, "Your brother will rise again."

Martha answered, "I know he will rise again in the resurrection at the last day."

Jesus said to her, "I am the resurrection and the life. He who believes in me will live, even though he dies; and whoever lives and believes in me will never die. Do you believe this?"

JOHN 11:17-26

Death puts life into proper perspective. For those who die, it's an immediate doorway to heaven or hell, but for those who remain it's like a window. What do you see as you peer through the dark glass? What are you going to do about it? My helplessness in the face of suffering and death will, sooner or later, either send me to my knees in prayer or plunge me into a whirlpool of bitterness and self-destruction.

Who's to Blame?

The jaundice was still faintly evident in his face. Obviously he had a liver condition.

On the phone his wife had cautioned me that Nick was extremely nervous and upset. She said he paced endlessly in a state of utter despair. And it was true. In fact, he greeted me at the door with almost open hostility. I seemed to be a symbol of the cause of his black depression.

Just twenty-four hours before, Nick had gotten the straightforward verdict—he had cancer of the liver. Not only was it terminal, but at best he had three months left. The doctor gave the diagnosis and issued the death warrant in the same stroke.

Nick was a Russian immigrant who carried within him all the native open, brutal honesty of his old culture. What he felt was what he said, loud and clear. He was mad, furious, distraught, and ready to heap revenge somewhere on someone for this visitation of tragedy.

"I'm going to die! Do you understand that? I am going to die, and they are going to put me in the ground. They are going to throw dirt on my face. Do you understand that? I'm dying right now!"

I nodded. My mind was racing to find something to say, but nothing seemed better than just letting the silence work.

"You're supposed to know about God. You're supposed

to talk to God. Why have I been picked to just get blown away? What have I done that was so bad that He should reach out to put an end to my life?"

I mustered up a timid counseling response: "You seem to feel God has done this to you?"

"*Seem* to feel? *Seem* to feel? Of course I do! Who else did this to me? If there's a God, I want to know why He's done this terrible thing to me, to my wife, to my family!"

And then he broke down into sobs of anguish.

Nick's plea of "why me" is representative of all humanity. In his despair, he felt that the source of his condition must be established. If he had been arbitrarily picked to go to the bone pile, then any words of pious comfort would be just sore lies. Unless he could see a satisfactory reason for his condition, there could be no comfort for him as he faced death.

That scene has been enacted a billion times. When our life is unexpectedly shortened, when our potential is wiped out, when our mate is left to face lonely days, we want an answer. Who is to blame for this? Who has done this to me?

ROBERT WISE[3]

In her exceptional and comprehensive *Mourning Handbook*, Helen Fitzgerald writes, "Anger and even rage are common reactions to the loss of a loved one. You may be terribly angry right now as you think about what you have lost and how your life has been changed overnight." And, she notes, you may be angry about a number of things:

- You may be angry with the hospital staff or the medical professionals for not responding quickly or appropriately.

- You may be angry with friends or relatives who, in their lack of understanding, or because they are caught up in their own grief, make comments that are not helpful.

- You may be angry at the person who dies and has left you behind, facing a lot of legal work and loneliness.

- You may be angry at yourself for not doing enough.

- You may be angry because of the change in life-style inflicted upon you.

- You may be angry over role changes that have to be made within your family.

- You may be angry for what you perceive to be a loss of control in your life.

- You may be angry that family and friends have gone back to their normal lives and aren't thinking about your grief.

- You may be angry that the rest of the world busies itself around you as though nothing has happened.

- You may be angry with God![4]

GOD ISN'T MAD BECAUSE YOU ARE

Anger, then, is the perfectly normal response to death, provided it doesn't get the best of you. It's also comforting to know that your anger will never get the best of God. I find the Psalms profoundly comforting in this regard. Not only does the psalmist say nice things about God, like "The Lord is my Shepherd, I shall not want," but he also makes appeals to God angrily,

> How long, O Lord? Will you forget me forever?
> How long will you hide your face from me?
> How long must I wrestle with my thoughts
> and every day have sorrow in my heart?
> How long will my enemy triumph over me?

Look on me and answer, O Lord my God.
Give light to my eyes, or I will sleep in death. PSALMS 13:1-3

Do you think God is horrified by your anger? That in the history of the human race he's never seen anyone get upset? It's not as if you can hide your anger from God anyway! You can pretend to be holy and gracious in God's presence, but you won't fool him. I have the feeling he would rather you had it out with him, not because he needs to know how you feel, but because you need to know how you feel.

The brutal honesty of the psalmist, recorded right there in God's holy book, assures me that God isn't even slightly miffed by my questions, or even by my anger, and I am comforted to know that my anger doesn't make God angry. If we cannot express ourselves freely in God's presence, what's the point of prayer? Is God less understanding than your pastor? Than your counselor? You mean you have the freedom to tell your therapist how you feel, but you can't tell God?

You *need* to talk about your anger. To God. To others who, like God, will listen without making judgments. At the same time, you have to realize that long-term, persistent anger is the worst thing you can do for yourself and others. Sooner or later, you need to ask for healing. Even King David ends his enraged prayer in Psalms 13:5-6 by confessing,

> **But** [in spite of how I feel,
> in spite of all my angry questions]
> I trust in your unfailing love;
> my heart rejoices in your salvation.
> I will sing to the Lord,
> for he has been good to me. PSALMS 13:5-6

Resentment Is Not a Requirement of Grief

When we say anger and resentment are a part of "good grief," we probably should qualify this to some extent. We do not wish to leave the impression that persons in grief ought to be encouraged to be angry or resentful. What we are saying is that these feelings are normal for every human, and that even the most devout persons can very well feel angry and resentful, even though we try very hard to sublimate these feelings. It would be most harmful to us if we could not admit to ourselves, to God, and to our friends that we, being human, need to confess our anger and resentfulness and ask for strength to rise above it.

Another way to put it is to say that resentment is not a healthy emotion and, if allowed to take over, it can be very, very harmful. Yet it is a normal part of the grief process. It is to be expected, it is to be wrestled with, and it can, by the grace of God, be overcome.

GRANGER WESTBERG[5]

EPHESIANS 4:26-27...

Be ye angry and sin not: let not the sun go down upon your wrath: Neither give place to the devil. *KING JAMES VERSION*

"In your anger do not sin." Do not let the sun go down while you are still angry, and do not give the devil a foothold.
NEW INTERNATIONAL VERSION

When angry, do not sin; do not ever let your wrath (your exasperation, your fury or indignation) last until the sun goes down. Leave no [such] room or foothold for the devil [give no opportunity to him]. *THE AMPLIFIED BIBLE*

If you are angry, be sure that it is not a sinful anger. Never go to bed angry—don't give the devil that sort of foothold.

J.B. PHILLIPS TRANSLATION

Go ahead and be angry. You do well to be angry—but don't use your anger as fuel for revenge. And don't stay angry. Don't go to bed angry. Don't give the Devil that kind of foothold in your life.

THE MESSAGE

Anger's Wicked Pleasure

Of the Seven Deadly Sins, anger is possibly the most fun. To lick your wounds, to smack your lips over grievances long past, to roll over your tongue the prospect of bitter confrontations still to come, to savor to the last toothsome morsel both the pain you are given and the pain you are giving back—in many ways it is a feast fit for a king. The chief drawback is that what you are wolfing down is yourself. The skeleton at the feast is you.

FREDERICK BUECHNER[6]

The acts of the sinful nature are obvious...fits of rage...But the fruit of the Spirit is love, joy, peace... GALATIANS 5:19-22

Peace I leave with you; my peace I give you. I do not give to you as the world gives. Do not let your hearts be troubled and do not be afraid. JOHN 14:27

DEPRESSION

I have had a family history of depression, so I know firsthand there are no easy answers. Depression is not just something you can make go away, and people who do not suffer from severe depression can be downright insensitive and impatient with those who do. "Just trust God," they tell us glibly. "Just try to snap out of it. You can do it!" But you can't. No matter how hard you try.

> *You have lost interest not only in yourself and those around you, but in life itself.*
>
> *As you are empty, so is the world around you.*
>
> *This depression is not weakness. It is a psychological necessity. It is one of the slow winding avenues of sorrow and loss. It is part of the mournful work of saying "Good-by" to your beloved.*
>
> EARL A. GROLLMAN[7]

Depression is painfully complex, although there are essentially only two kinds of depression: "acute," which is the direct consequence of a traumatic loss, and "chronic," which is long-lived, unremitting, and unexplainable melancholy. Everyone at one time or another will experience depression, particularly the acute kind. Depression happens. Especially when someone you love dies. *Depression is how you feel when your anger over your loss turns outside in.* Depression is how you feel because you feel so left behind and lonely.

Endless Neverness

It's the *neverness* that is so painful. *Never again* to be here with us—never to sit with us at table, never to travel with us, never to laugh with us, never to cry with us, never to embrace us as he leaves for school, never to see his brothers and sister marry. All the rest of our lives we must live without him. Only our death can stop the pain of death.

A month, a year, five years—with that I could live. But not this forever.

I step outdoors into the moist moldy fragrance of an early summer morning and arm in arm with my enjoyment comes the realization that never again will he smell this.

As a cloud vanishes and is gone,
so he who goes down to the grave
does not return.
He will never come to his house again;
his place will know him no more. JOB 7:9-10

One small misstep and now this endless neverness.

NICHOLAS WOLTERSTORFF[8]

Chronic depression is particularly difficult to overcome because you aren't sure why you feel so terrible. You just do. One explanation, and it's a valid one, is that chronic depression can be physiological. To put it simply, it's the result of a chemical problem in the brain, so doctors prescribe a variety of anti-depressants, some of which have helped people immensely. Drugs can be a temporary remedy in profoundly difficult times, and they can bring some long-term relief for people who have serious chemical imbalances.

If you are severely depressed, if you feel like your depression is getting the best of you, consult with your physician. And if you are in any way feeling suicidal on the deep end of your depression, get help immediately. Like right now. Call somebody before you finish this chapter.

But don't leave God out of the prescription. At some point, each of us has to take some responsibility for our feelings and emotions. The Bible has a lot to say about peace of mind. Here is one of the better known passages:

> As the deer pants for streams of water,
> so my soul pants for you, O God.
> My soul thirsts for God, for the living God.
> When can I go and meet with God?
> My tears have been my food day and night,
> while men say to me all day long,
> "Where is your God?"
> These things I remember
> as I pour out my soul:
> how I used to go with the multitude,
> leading the procession to the house of God,
> with shouts of joy and thanksgiving
> among the festive throng.
>
> Why are you downcast, O my soul?
> Why so disturbed within me?
> Put your hope in God,
> for I will yet praise him,
> my Savior and my God.
> My soul is downcast within me....
>
> I say to God my Rock,
> "Why have you forgotten me?
> Why must I go about mourning,
> oppressed by the enemy?"
> My bones suffer mortal agony
> as my foes taunt me,
> saying to me all day long,
> "Where is your God?"

Why are you downcast, O my soul?
Why so disturbed within me?
Put your hope in God,
for I will yet praise him,
my Savior and my God. PSALMS 42

CONFRONTING THE SPIRIT OF DEPRESSION

John and Margie Dalton have been my companions in the process of writing this book as they have shared with me in depth and at length about their own grief in the loss of their children. On healing the grieving, John asks,

How do we deal with grieving, as family and friends go through their stages of grief? Only recently have I had any sense of how this would be accomplished. It seems to me that the first high energy stage of grief needs comforters. The second low energy stage needs intercessors, and the third stage of gradual return of energy requires challengers.

When an acquaintance of mine, Pastor Bob (not his real name), was dying of liver cancer in a California hospital, some Christian friends from another church drove a great distance to minister to him. They found him withdrawn, uncommunicative, and unwilling to participate in any dialogue. He just wanted to be left to die in isolation. He was, as I see it, in the low energy stage of his own grief process, a stage that may well have opened his heart to spiritual oppression.

His friends honored his request to be left alone but determined to persist in prayer and refused to leave the hospital. Turning the visitors' lounge into a spiritual war room, they prayed against the spiritual oppression gripping Bob's soul. After several days of fervent intercession, the power of the depression was broken, and Bob, emerging from his despair, invited his friends back into his hospital room. There they spent the next several days in worship and praise, reading the Bible and praying. And then he died. In peace.

This story has meant so much to me, because it points out

how grief creates its own prison of lonely isolation, how the devil himself can take advantage of our emotional vulnerability, and how we can be set free through the guidance and power of the Holy Spirit. I have also learned how sensitive Christians can intervene in "the heavenlies" in a kind of spiritual therapy for the person who is suffering severe depression.

Perhaps this is why the apostle Paul urges Christians to put on the full armor of God, specifically the helmet of salvation.[9] In my book *Overcoming the Dominion of Darkness*, I have made a strong case for the possibility of Satan's direct influence on the minds of emotionally vulnerable and unsuspecting people. "I am afraid," Paul writes, "that just as Eve was deceived by the serpent's cunning [a fairly obvious reference to the devil!], your minds may somehow be led astray from your sincere and pure devotion to Christ" (2 Corinthians 11:3).

Depression is caused by loss. It is a child of grief, a brother of anger, and a cousin of loneliness. It may also be deepened by dark spirits. I realize this book is not essentially about what many refer to as "spiritual warfare," but an honest discussion of depression cannot leave out this element, because what you believe about depression will determine how you treat it. So treat it realistically. Maybe you need to treat it with medication, at least for a while. The kind of medication you need must be prescribed by a doctor. But above all, treat depression with prayer:

> Our Father,
> Who art in heaven,
> Hallowed be thy name.
>
> Thy kingdom come.
> Thy will be done
> on earth,
> as it is in heaven.
>
> Give us this day
> our daily bread.

And forgive us our debts,
as we forgive our debtors.

**And lead us not into temptation,
but deliver us from evil**
[literally, "from the evil one"].

For thine is the kingdom,
and the power,
and the glory,
forever and ever, *Amen.*

In conclusion be strong—not in yourselves but in the Lord, in
the power of his boundless strength. Put on God's complete
armor so that you can successfully resist all the devil's craftiness.
For our fight is not against any physical enemy; we are up
against the unseen power that controls this dark world, and spiritual agents from the very headquarters of evil. Therefore you
must wear the whole armor of God that you may be able to
resist evil in its day of power, and that even when you have
fought to a standstill you may still stand your ground. Take your
stand then with truth as your belt, integrity your breastplate, the
gospel of peace firmly on your feet, salvation as your helmet and
in your hand the sword of the Spirit, the Word of God. Above
all be sure you take faith as your shield, for it can quench every
burning missile the enemy hurls at you.

EPHESIANS 6:10-16, PHILLIPS[10]

SIX

Well-Meaning People, Witless Wisdom
Countering Negative Input

But now, Job, listen to my words;
pay attention to everything I say...
My words come from an upright heart;
my lips sincerely speak what I know.

ELIHU, JOB'S COUNSELOR,
JOB 33:1, 3

The Old Testament book of Job is about suffering, as in "Job-like suffering." It's also a book about well-meaning people who say really inappropriate things. Most of the people in your life have your best interests at heart and they truly want to say something constructive.

It is inevitable, though, that a lot of those people will say trite and insensitive things. Occasionally you'll even catch yourself thinking, *Now that was a stupid thing to say.* But you'll smile and thank them for their concern.

Other times you may not know what to think, because your friends are dedicated Christians, people whom you respect. Elihu and Job's other counselors, Eliphaz, Bildad, and Zophar, sat with Job for seven days *without saying a word.* I wish I could say that about some of the people who have given me unsolicited advice.

When Job's friends first saw him, "they began to weep aloud, and they tore their robes and sprinkled dust on their heads. Then they sat on the ground with him for seven days and seven nights. *No one said a word to him,* because they saw how great his suffering was" (Job 2:12-13).

Would that some of our friends were so devoted to our comfort and healing! Yet these wise men still missed the mark. Try as they would, they could not explain Job's unexplainable loss, and they ended up saying things that did more harm than good. Dave Murrow, who lost his son, wrote to me,

I struggle to understand where God fits into all this. I'm not to the point that I can even have realistic prayer and dialogue with him about it. I start to speak to the Lord in rational fashion and end up crying out, "Oh, Jesus!" I cannot seem to get into the deep philosophical stuff with God just now—maybe later.

God has a special plan in store for those Christian friends who tell you that everything would have worked out all right if only I had had more faith. "Vengeance is mine," says the Lord. But I would love to be there to watch.

People come to us all the time and try to comfort us. Usually they say something like, "I understand your pain." Or, "I know what you're going through." The truth is, if they haven't lost a child of their own, they probably don't have a clue.

A Christian writer and pastor friend of mine, Roy Lawson, lost his oldest son to suicide two years ago. He wrote:

What I struggled with in those early days following Lane's death was the inescapable fact that he had *chosen* to die. This young man, so loved and so vibrant when feeling well, so gifted and giving, had turned his back on life.

Well wishers, hoping to ease our pain, spoke or wrote authoritatively of God's will in the matter. God must have somehow willed Lane's death, or wanted Lane in heaven with him, or felt Lane's work on earth was done. Some even mused on how God would enhance my ministry through this "sacrifice." Rather than giving me peace, these words added to my confusion. After all, we had prayed God's protection on our son, entrusting this precious life into God's providential hands.

Had God been responsible for his death?

No, that couldn't be the answer. I gradually came to see that the God who respects human individuality enough to allow us to refuse his love—who *bids* us come but never commands us to be saved against our will—respected Lane's choice of death over painful life.

Lane didn't die because God failed to answer our prayers or watch over our son; he didn't seek God's counsel in the matter. Instead, he listened to his pain and was persuaded. I'm convinced God was as heartbroken over his decision as we were, and much more understanding than I. So with his mother, I commended him to the love of his heavenly Father, and found peace.

And Judy Hawk, who lost her grown son several years ago, wrote to me:

A friend of ours approached my husband and me at the visitation, put his arms around us—he really cared—and then proceeded to quote Romans 8:28. You've probably heard it before, perhaps during a difficult time in your life: "All things work together for good for those who love God."

I could see the anger in my husband's face, and I gently led him away to keep him from punching our well-intentioned friend.

Sharing Scripture with someone who is grieving certainly has its place, but friends should be very selective in their choice of Bible verses. And waiting a few weeks—and for just the right moment—will make God's Word more meaningful to the grieving.

I am inclined, however, to advise people *never* to use Romans 8:28 shortly after a death, because it is often next to impossible for the bereaved to see any good in the passing of their loved one. For my husband and me, we found that it took a good while before Romans 8:28 made sense in our loss. No Bible verse will take the hurt away, until a person can see it with God's intervention and help.

People may give you bad advice with good intentions. They may even quote Scripture when you least want to hear it. But you have to know that you are a bit of the problem. Not that your faith has failed, or that you are guilty in some way. But right now you're so vulnerable. You are looking for explanations. Any explanation. The look on your face pleads, "Say something. Please help me understand. What do *you* think about all this?"

So they tell you.

Worse, they might sincerely believe that what they think about your situation is really what *God* thinks.

And then there are people who won't say anything. They have no idea what to say, so they just smile while you stare into their blank expressions and try desperately to figure out what they're thinking.

Or maybe they refuse to make eye contact with you, or even shy away from you altogether. Margie Dalton wrote to me,

People would avoid us. If one of us was walking down the street, people would deliberately cross over to the other side so they wouldn't have to speak with us.

We understood. What do you say to someone who has lost three children?

On the other hand, there would be those whose words came easily as they quoted Scripture and theorized about God's grace in a situation like ours.

I would have rather been alone. What I needed were friends who would put some meat on the bones of their ideas and explanations: to scrub the floor when I had no energy or motivation to do it myself; to iron a shirt for John when I didn't have the heart to do it; to love my surviving children by taking them to the park, or by baking them a chocolate cake when I didn't have the emotional strength to do even that.

MORALIZING

Asking why and ascribing guilt. It's what people seem compelled to do whenever there's a human tragedy.

"Why did this happen?"

"What is the deeper meaning?"

"How does God fit into all of this?"

We all moralize about nearly everything, but we do it especially when someone dies. I've done it, even though I've taught people in my congregation not to do it. Job's counselors did it. The disciples of Jesus did it:

As [Jesus] went along, he saw a man blind from birth. His disciples asked him, "Rabbi, who sinned, this man or his parents, that he was born blind?"

"Neither this man nor his parents sinned," said Jesus, "but this happened so that the work of God might be displayed in his life." JOHN 9:1-3

So many things in God's creation have a cause-and-effect relationship that we assume some spiritual or moral explanation underlies every human tragedy. Obviously, one person's death (*the effect*) may have been the result of another person's negligent or drunk driving (*the cause*).

But the deeper question is always, "Why this victim? Why not some other victim? Why did this happen when it happened? To *my* loved one?" If only the circumstances had been slightly different, maybe the person you loved would not have died.

Earlier this evening I was yelling and screaming at a Phoenix Suns basketball game. Just two weeks ago tonight my daughter Shari and my son Matthew had tickets to a Suns game too, but they never got there. As she exited the freeway on her way to the arena, Shari collided with another car. In a flash their evening was ruined.

I shamed myself: "If only I had not given them the tickets..."

My daughter Shari agonized, "I should never have planned to go to the game tonight."

Later, I found myself wondering if perhaps it was because I had not been praying as much lately.

And a week later I goaded my friend who gave me the tickets in the first place, "Hey, if you hadn't offered me the tickets, my daughter wouldn't have wrecked my car!" Laughing at me, he protested, "You're not going to lay any guilt on me!"

All in good humor? No subtle messages of responsibility exchanged?

Why did it happen? Did my kids sin, or was it the sin of their father and mother? Or was it the guy who gave me the tickets to the game? Or the guy who gave him the tickets?

"Who sinned, this man or his parents, that he was born blind?"

Gratefully, no one was injured in the collision. It wasn't even close to the kind of loss some of you readers have suffered, but I still found myself evaluating the ageless questions about God, sin, and guilt.

Moralizing. It can be downright demoralizing.

Life Comes in Fragments

Once there was an old man who lived in a tiny village. Although poor, he was envied by all, for he owned a beautiful white horse. Even the king coveted his treasure. A horse like this had never been seen before—such was its splendor, its majesty, its strength.

People offered fabulous prices for the steed, but the old man always refused. "This horse is not a horse to me," he would tell them. "It is a person. How could you sell a person? He is a friend, not a possession. How could you sell a friend?" The man was poor and the temptation was great. But he never sold the horse.

One morning he found that the horse was not in the stable. All the village came to see him. "You old fool," they scoffed, "we told you that someone would steal your horse. We warned you that you would be robbed. You are so poor. How could you ever hope to protect such a valuable animal? It would have been better to have sold him. You could have gotten whatever price you wanted. No amount would have been too high. Now the horse is gone, and you've been cursed with misfortune."

The old man responded, "Don't speak too quickly. Say only that the horse is not in the stable. That is all we know; the rest is judgment. If I've been cursed or not, how can you know? How can you judge?"

The people contested, "Don't make us out to be fools! We may not be philosophers, but great philosophy is not needed. The simple fact that your horse is gone is a curse."

The old man spoke again, "All I know is that the stable is empty, and the horse is gone. The rest I don't know. Whether it be a curse or a blessing, I can't say. All we can see is a fragment. Who can say what will come next?"

The people of the village laughed. They thought that the man was crazy. They had always thought he was a fool; if he wasn't, he would have sold the horse and lived off the money. But instead, he was a poor woodcutter, an old man still cutting firewood and dragging it out of the forest and selling it. He lived hand to mouth in the misery of poverty. Now he had proven that he was, indeed, a fool.

After fifteen days, the horse returned. He hadn't been stolen; he had run away into the forest. Not only had he returned, he had brought a dozen wild horses with him. Once again the village people gathered around the woodcutter and spoke. "Old man, you were right and we were wrong. What we thought was a curse was a blessing. Please forgive us."

The man responded, "Once again, you go too far. Say only that the horse is back. State only that a dozen horses returned with him, but don't judge. How do you know if this is a blessing or not? You only see a fragment. Unless you know the whole story, how can you judge? You read only one page of a book. Can you judge the whole book? You read only one word of a phrase. Can you understand the entire phrase?

"Life is so vast, yet you judge all of life with one page or one word. All you have is a fragment! Don't say that this is a blessing. No one knows. I am content with what I know. I am not perturbed by what I don't."

"Maybe the old man is right," they said to one another. So they said little. But down deep, they knew he was wrong. They knew it was a blessing. Twelve wild horses had returned with one horse. With a little bit of work, the animals could be broken and trained and sold for much money.

The old man had a son, an only son. The young man began to break the wild horses. After a few days, he fell from one of the horses and broke both legs. Once again the villagers gathered around the old man and cast their judgments.

"You were right," they said. "You proved you were right. The dozen horses were not a blessing. They were a curse. Your son has broken his legs, and now in your old age you have no one to help you. Now you are poorer than ever."

The old man spoke again. "You people are obsessed with judging. Don't go so far. Say only that my son broke his legs. Who knows if it is a blessing or curse? No one knows. We only have a fragment. Life comes in fragments."

It so happened that a few weeks later the country engaged in war against a neighboring country. All the young men of the village were required to join the army. Only the son of the old man was excluded, because he was injured. Once again the people gathered around the old man, crying and screaming because their sons had been taken. There was little chance they would return. The enemy was strong, and the war would be a losing struggle. They would never see their sons again.

"You were right, old man," they wept. "God knows you were right. This proves it. Your son's accident was a blessing. His legs may be broken, but at least he is with you. Our sons are gone forever."

The old man spoke again. "It is impossible to talk with you. You always draw conclusions. No one knows. Say only this: Your sons had to go to war, and mine did not. No one knows if it is a blessing or a curse. No one is wise enough to know. Only God knows."

MAX LUCADO[1]

For we know in part and we prophesy in part, but when perfection comes, the imperfect disappears... Now we see but a poor reflection; then we shall see face to face. Now I know in part; then I shall know fully, even as I am fully known.

And now these three remain: faith, hope, and love. But the greatest of these is love. 1 CORINTHIANS 13:9-13

Now we have to be honest. Some tragedies are indeed the direct consequence of sin. I also believe that every loss is a window to heaven that drives us to search our souls—and our relationship with

God. That's good. (I'm going to talk about all of this in much more detail in chapter thirteen: "Unsolved Mysteries.")

But searching *too* deeply is an exercise in mental and spiritual futility, especially in the early weeks and months following the death of a loved one. Others will do it for you, whether or not you ask them, so be kind to yourself. Try hard to leave the difficult questions for later. For some answers, you will probably have to wait until you get to heaven.

Insufferable Friends

[Job] had four well-meaning but insufferable friends who came over to cheer him up and try to explain [his suffering]. They said that anybody with enough sense to come in out of the rain knew that God was just. They said that anybody old enough to spell his own name knew that since God was just, he made bad things happen to bad people and good things happen to good people. They said that such being the case, you didn't need a Harvard diploma to figure out that since bad things had happened to Job, then *ipso facto* he must have done something bad himself. But Job hadn't, and he said so, and that's not all he said either. "Worthless physicians are you all," he said. "Oh that you would keep silent, and it would be your wisdom" (Job 13:4-5). They were a bunch of theological quacks, in other words, and the smartest thing they could do was shut up. But they were too busy explaining things to listen.

FREDERICK BUECHNER[2]

Enough Clichés to Last a Lifetime

Moralizing can be disguised as deep spiritual wisdom, as in the case of Job's friends. Clichés, on the other hand, are for people who want to moralize but don't want to think, so they just blurt out superficial, untimely bits of unproven popular wisdom. Stuff that sounds wise but isn't. Witless wisdom. Never forget that people mean well, although knowing that may or may not ease your frustration and pain.

Erin Linn, who has written an entire book on witless wisdom, has cleverly categorized some of the more common clichés:

"Be Strong" Clichés

Big boys don't cry.
The children are flexible...
　　they will bounce back.
You must be strong for the children.
Support groups are for wimps.
You've just got to get a hold of yourself!
Others have held up well. You can too.
Cheer up.
No sense crying over spilt milk.
This is nature's way.

"Hurry Up" Clichés

You're not your old self.
Out of sight, out of mind.
Time will heal.
You're young, and you will be able
　　to make a new life for yourself.
I just don't understand your behavior.
Life goes on.
No sense dwelling on the past.

"GUILT" CLICHÉS

If you look around, you can always find someone who is worse off than yourself.

This is the work of the devil (which means that if you had a closer relationship with God, the devil could not have had his way).

If I were you, I would do it this way.

Count your blessings.

Only the good die young.

If you had been a better Christian, this would not have happened to you.

Think of all your precious memories.

It's a blessing.

"GOD" CLICHÉS

God needs him more than you do.

He is happy now, because he's with God.

God did this to show how powerful he can be in your life.

It was God's will.

God never gives us more than we can handle.

God helps those who help themselves.

"DISCOUNT" CLICHÉS

I know just how you feel.

Silence is golden.

If there is anything I can do, just call me.

You can have more children.

It's better to have loved and lost
than never to have loved at all.

Be glad you don't have problems like mine.

What you don't know, won't hurt you.[3]

The apostle Paul seemed to recognize this problem when he addressed the Corinthians: "I am not writing this to shame you, but to warn you, as my dear children. *Even though you have ten thousand guardians in Christ, you do not have many fathers,* for in Christ Jesus I became your father through the gospel (emphasis added)."[4]

In other words, every man on the street will give you free advice, even when he doesn't know what he's talking about and often without you having to ask. In fact, most people *like* to give counsel, but not everyone has the empathy and patience of a good father. Though we don't like to admit it, most of us just don't know what to say in life's darker moments.

So what do you do? Well, first you need to read and reread books like this one! Nobody's perfect, but men and women who write on grief are generally well-informed on the ins and outs of what people feel and experience during a time of loss. There are many excellent books on grief work, and you should probably make the effort to read more than one or two. Different authors will approach the subject from different perspectives, which is helpful. Also, reading good books will help you sort through all the witless wisdom.

Second, you need to talk with someone knowledgeable and skilled in working with people in grief. Additionally, there are growing numbers of support groups, some of which are very needs-specific. At our church, for example, we have a grief support group for parents of murdered children.

For leads, you can call your local hospital, the hospital chaplain's office, a local counseling center, and, of course, your local church. Most clergy, because they are asked to do funerals and are appropriately trained, have an accurate perspective on grief and loss. It may surprise you, though, to know that some churches, including some pastors and not a few good Christians, are not so well prepared to help you through the maze of grief.

I know. I'm a pastor. I've said and done some really dumb things myself.

On the one hand, you need to go for help to people you love and trust the most; on the other hand, you need to be realistic. Not everyone you love and trust will know how to handle your loss and everything you're going through emotionally.

If this chapter makes you angry, or if it reminds you of people who have made you angry, go back to the last chapter, "So You're Mad?"

Maybe you bounce back and forth between anger and the condemnation you feel because there is always an element of truth in witless wisdom. That's why the next chapter is about guilt.

SEVEN

If Only I Had...
Guilt and Forgiveness

When death comes, life is examined.

EARL A. GROLLMAN

When somebody you've wronged forgives you, you're spared the dull and self-diminishing throb of a guilty conscience. When you forgive somebody who has wronged you, you're spared the dismal corrosion of bitterness and wounded-pride.

FREDERICK BUECHNER

The call came at an inconvenient time. They always do. A young couple in our church was expecting a child, but not three months early.

"Pastor Gary, would you come to the hospital to pray for us?" Jim asked.

The birth of a baby is supposed to be a happy time, but Jim and Beth's third child had such severe genetic disfigurement that, before anyone else from their family came to visit and see their little boy, they wanted prayer and spiritual counsel.

I can still see Beth's weary face. Having a child is difficult enough for a mom, but now this. As our eyes met, Beth could not have looked more sad.

"Do you think this was caused by something wrong in my life?"

That was her first question! Was something wrong with her?! I reassured her that no, absolutely not, this was not her fault, but I could tell she was not immediately convinced.

It's just human nature to feel guilty. Because we are. The apostle Paul admitted, "For what I want to do I do not do, but what I hate, I do.... I know that nothing good lives in me, that is, in my sinful nature. For I have the desire to do what is good, but I cannot carry it out.... When I want to do good, evil is right there with me.... What a wretched man I am! Who will rescue me from this body of death?" (Romans 7:15-24).

The fact is, we do a lot of things we regret, and there are many other things we have neglected to do, things we wish we had done. So when something terrible happens, especially when a loved one dies, all of the worst feelings we have about ourselves emerge, and we feel so guilty. It's not necessarily right or wrong. It's just the way it is. For everybody.

I mentioned earlier in this book that my mother, in her own home, is caring for my grandmother, who has been bedridden for nearly two years. My mother gave the same tender care to her father, who passed away some years ago. Did she do enough? Absolutely! But a day or two after my grandfather died, my mother asked through her tears, "I just wonder if there was something else I could have done."

Not only can you feel guilty about the way you failed your deceased loved one, you can even feel guilty about how you have handled your guilt and grief. Margie Dalton wrote to me:

Both my husband and I were afraid to show our intense grief for fear that once the tears began again they would never end. It has taken years for us to be able to forgive one another for all the deficits of relationship that occurred, to begin to relate again in healthy and real ways.

God in his grace brought others alongside, others who in the name of Jesus could touch our need for deep healing. I had to forgive God for allowing Tom to die. I had to forgive Tom for dying. I had to give up the "if onlys" and the "what ifs" and begin to allow God in his love and grace to speak to my profound hurt.

Guilt

"If only I had...

*treated the one I loved
more kindly.*

called the doctor sooner.

*understood the full extent
of the illness.*

*taken better care of
him or her.*

not lost my temper.

*expressed my affection
more frequently."*

*When death comes, life is
examined.*

*You become acutely aware of
your failures, real or imagined.
You want to rectify past errors.*

You wish to compensate for
the wrongs you have committed.

Some people even punish themselves
with self-destructive acts,
as if to say: "See how much
I am suffering. Doesn't this
prove my great love?"

Self-recrimination becomes a way
to undo all the things that
make you now feel guilty.

And maybe you were guilty.
Perhaps you said things you
should not have said.
Perhaps you neglected to do things
you should have done.
But who hasn't?

What is past is past.
It cannot be changed.
You already have too much pain
to add to the burden of self-
accusation, self-reproach, and
self-depreciation.

EARL A. GROLLMAN[1]

SINNERS FEEL GUILTY

Some believe that guilt is a social problem, or even a religious problem. In other words, the reason people feel guilty is because other people, especially religious people, make them feel guilty. But guilt is a sin problem.

Guilt and sin are first cousins. Like sin, guilt is an inseparable part of the human condition. Guilt is "normal." Yet guilt is not something you have to live with. Like sin, you have to face its reality, but you don't have to accept it. And like sin, guilt is something that can only be fully healed through relationship with God. Guilt comes from sin—real and imagined. Healing comes from God.

Perhaps people are telling you that you have no reason to feel guilty, and you know they're right. Mostly. But deep inside, you still know something is wrong. You could have done more. And you did some things you really regret. In fact, maybe there are some memories or feelings about the person who died that you don't feel you can share with anyone, because they are, frankly, so sinful.

God has to forgive you before you can forgive yourself. Why don't you close your eyes, right now, and pray a couple of times, "Our Father in heaven, forgive me. Heal my pain. Take away my guilt."

If we refuse to admit that we are sinners, then we live in a world of illusion and truth becomes a stranger to us. But if we freely admit that we have sinned, we find him reliable and just—he forgives our sins and makes us thoroughly clean from all that is evil.

1 JOHN 1:8-9, PHILLIPS

EXPERIENCING THE FORGIVENESS OF GOD

We need to talk about the two most important words in the verse above: *sin* and *forgiveness*. Generally, sin is what you do wrong and what you don't do right, but the New Testament Greek term used here is *hamartia*, which refers simply to missing the mark or falling short.

Human sin can express itself in the ugliest, nastiest, most wicked ways, but it's also everything about us that always falls just a little short of what we ought to be. Like not calling your mother often enough. Or when you do, not talking long enough. Or not being more genuinely interested when she is talking. As my friend Dean Sherman of Youth With A Mission says, "We just don't do all the right things at all the right times for all the right reasons."

It would be easy to say, "Nobody's perfect," as though that will take away the guilt. It's true. *Nobody* is perfect. But it's also true that everyone feels guilty, and we can't just talk ourselves out of our guilt. Guilt is directly related to sin, to missing the mark, to falling short. Unless we heal the cause of guilt, the guilt just isn't going to go away, which brings us to the second important word in 1 John 1:8-9: *forgiveness.*

The New Testament Greek word translated "forgive" means "to release," *to let go.* One New Testament study guide notes that forgiveness "is the voluntary release of a person or thing over which one has legal or actual control." Originally, the word was used to describe the release of a ship from its moorings, that is, when a ship is released to set sail, it has been "forgiven." In early Greek literature, this term was also used to describe the release of an arrow. An arrow on a drawn bowstring is under tension. Release the tension and the arrow is "forgiven."[2]

"Look, the Lamb of God!" proclaimed John the Baptist. "[He is the one] who takes away the sin of the world" (John 1:29). There's that word *sin* again, and what does Jesus do about it? He takes it away. He doesn't talk it away. He doesn't just overlook it. He takes it away. He *releases* us from the power of sin and its consequences. That's forgiveness.

> The Lord is compassionate and gracious,
> slow to anger, abounding in love.
> He will not always accuse,
> nor will he harbor his anger forever;
> **he does not treat us as our sins deserve**
> **or repay us according to our iniquities.**
>
> For as high as the heavens are above the earth,
> so great is his love for those
> who fear him.
> **As far as the east is from the west,**
> **so far has he removed our transgressions**
> **from us.**
>
> As a father has compassion on his children,
> so the Lord has compassion on those
> who fear him;
> for he knows how we are formed,
> he remembers that we are dust. PSALMS 103:8-14

When God forgives you, he releases you from sin's entrapment *and guilt*. To be able to forgive yourself, you need to know that God has forgiven you. You only feel guilty for the failures you can remember, but God forgives you even for the failures you have forgotten. If we confess our failings, God is faithful and fair, and will release us from sin and guilt, even though he knows more about your failure than you do.

FORGIVING YOURSELF

I can defend myself. I can justify my behaviors. Or if I know I have done something wrong, I can minimize it. Or I can live in denial. But I can never fully forgive myself, at least not in the biblical sense. This is probably why denial is so enslaving, because it's the only way I can deal with my sin apart from God's help. I just pretend I don't have a problem, and before you know it, my pretending has become my reality.

So we're back to where we started: God. When God forgives me, I can forgive me. This is why the apostle Paul declares, "Therefore, there is now no condemnation for those who are in Christ Jesus, because through Christ Jesus the law of the Spirit of life set me free from the law of sin and death" (Romans 8:1-2).

Therefore, brothers, since we have confidence to enter the Most Holy Place by the blood of Jesus, by a new and living way opened for us through the curtain, that is, his body, and since we have a great priest over the house of God, let us draw near to God with a sincere heart in full assurance of faith, having our hearts sprinkled **to cleanse us from a guilty conscience.**

HEBREWS 10:19-22

The blood of Jesus cleanses me from all sin and releases me from my guilty conscience. But there's more. Sometimes, because our sins usually involve other people, it's necessary for us to go public. If there is anything we can do to heal ourselves, it's admitting to others our failure and pain.

"Confess your sins to each other," James pleads, "and pray for each other so that you may be healed. The prayer of a righteous man is powerful and effective" (James 5:16). After talking to God about your failure and guilt, talk to somebody else, and ask him or her to pray for you. The next best thing to God's forgiving and accepting us is when others accept us the way we are, even when we disclose to them our worst failings.

Sometimes it's almost as though guilt has a life of its own, because it keeps you from doing the very thing that will release you from its grip: confessing your sin to God and others. I'm not Roman Catholic, but I understand the power of the confessional. As a pastor, I've heard it all. People don't exactly come to me to confess in the same way they would confess to a Catholic priest, but the concerns and dynamics are identical.

When I demonstrate love, acceptance, and forgiveness to those who come to me with profound needs, they leave my office feeling released. And I understand why. I'm representing God. They can't talk to God directly, but they can talk to me, and they think of me as speaking for the Lord Jesus. When I forgive them, they have a deep sense that God has forgiven them.

When I announce, during the celebration of the Lord's Table, that everyone's sins are forgiven because of what Jesus has done, people actually *feel* forgiven. It's God speaking through me.

If you are Catholic, go confess your sins and sense of failure to your priest. If you are a Protestant, ask your pastor or an elder in your church to pray for you. In either case, make a point of going to Mass or "taking Communion." Do it many times if necessary, and allow each moment of confession, prayer, and communion with God to be one more step in the healing of your grief. God has forgiven you, but you need to know that. And you need to forgive yourself.

FORGIVING OTHERS

I'm not sure what is more difficult: forgiving yourself or forgiving others. Actually, they're interrelated: "Forgive us *our* sins," Jesus taught us to pray, "*as* we forgive the sins of *others*." Now this doesn't mean that God is waiting for us to forgive before he forgives us. If this were the correct way to read the Lord's Prayer, then we would have to conclude that salvation is not by grace alone.

Frederick Buechner writes, "Jesus is *not* saying that God's forgiveness is conditional upon our forgiving others. In the first place, forgiveness that's conditional isn't really forgiveness at all, just fair warning, and in the second place our unforgiveness is among those things about us which we need to have God forgive the most. What Jesus apparently *is* saying is that the pride which keeps us from forgiving is the same pride which keeps us from accepting forgiveness, and will God please help us do something about it."[3]

Jesus *is* telling us, then, that there is an inseparable link between forgiving others and receiving the forgiveness of God. When you refuse to forgive, God will not take back his forgiveness for you, but you will sure begin to wonder. Unforgiveness is like a dark cloud. It gets harder and harder to see God. In fact, it gets harder to see anything clearly.

If you cannot free people from their wrongs and see them as the needy people they are, you enslave yourself to your own painful past and by fastening yourself to the past, you let your hate become your future.

LEWIS SMEDES[4]

But how can I forgive? you wonder with genuine concern. Well, forgiveness, I'm sorry to say, can't be reduced to a "how-to," but there are some things you need to know. Or maybe you just need a reminder.

Your feelings of resentment are probably as diverse as the people in your life. You may have unresolved issues with the person who died. Maybe that person was abusive, but you still loved them. Or perhaps you're uncontrollably angry about someone who was responsible for the death. The other driver. A negligent doctor or health care worker. A murderer.

Eric was murdered. And they didn't find his body for two weeks. Eric's father, Paul, graciously agreed to share his story of anger, unforgiveness, and resolve....

Eric and I had not been getting along very well, so when Eric was first reported missing, I felt like God said to me, "I'll give you a second chance."

But when, after two weeks, Eric was found dead, I became confused. Didn't I hear from God? Was I making it up? Why did this happen? Why did God let us down? And I got angry with God. Extremely angry.

On my way home from work I would avoid most of the rush hour traffic by driving the country roads across the sparsely populated Pima Indian community. Early mornings and dark nights would find me in this remote area, where I felt safe to cry and even yell at God. "You can separate the waters of the Red Sea," I protested, "but you can't keep a gun from going off? You made the sun stand still, but you did nothing for my son."

In all my verbal badgering of God, not once did a lightning bolt even come close to me! Never did I hear, "Hey, do you know who you're yelling at?"

Then one day, in the darkness of that lonely, empty road that seemed so much like my life, I screamed, "God! My son is dead! My son died! Do you care?"

I'll never forget what I heard and felt within me at that moment: "I know exactly how you feel," God said, in my heart. "My Son died too."

Almost miraculously, I stopped crying, and a heavenly calm stayed with me the rest of the way home. No, I wasn't healed forever, but that moment helped me realize that God really did know how I felt. The heavenly Father experienced the same pain when his only Son Jesus died.

But as the days went by, I found myself arguing with God again. "Yeah, sure, your Son died too, but you raised him up from the dead," I shouted. To which God replied, "And I raised your son, too."

Again, suddenly, that same sense of peace came over me as I thought to myself—and it was *so* real to me, "My son, Eric, has seen Jesus Christ."

Some time later, my family and I attended a Parents of Murdered Children support group, where I met a man who was so angry and bitter that when I spoke to him, he would not even look me in the eye. His face was red with torment, even though it had been five years since he lost his daughter. It hit me that the perpetrator of the crime had not only taken the life of his child but had ruined his life as well. I knew right then, I didn't want to end up that way.

When you read Paul's story, it's evident that forgiveness cannot be reduced to a "how-to." How do you forgive the unforgivable? How do you forgive God?

Recently, I was gripped by a newspaper article about the fiftieth anniversary of the liberation of Auschwitz, where a million or more people were gassed and incinerated by the Nazis. Nobel Peace Prize-winner Elie Wiesel, a survivor of the death camp, prayed, "God of forgiveness, do not forgive those murderers of Jewish children here."

What do you think of that prayer?

What do you think of this prayer?....

> Appoint an evil man to oppose him;
> > let an accuser stand at his right hand.
> When he is tried, let him be found guilty,
> > and may his prayers condemn him.
> May his days be few....

> May his children be fatherless
> > and his wife a widow.
> May his children be wandering beggars;
> > may they be driven from their ruined homes.
> May a creditor seize all he has;
> > may strangers plunder the fruits of his labor.
> May no one extend kindness to him
> > or take pity on his fatherless children.
> May his descendants be cut off,
> > their names blotted out from the next generation.

> May the iniquity of his fathers be remembered
> before the Lord;
> may the sin of his mother never be blotted out.
> May their sins always remain before the Lord,
> that he may cut off the memory of them from
> the earth. PSALMS 109:6-15

I know that Christians are not supposed to pray like this. Or even think like this, because Jesus said, "You have heard that it was said, 'Eye for eye, and tooth for tooth.' But I tell you, Do not resist an evil person" (Matthew 5:38-39). And yet I'm grateful that the Bible, God's Holy Word, includes a few unholy prayers. It tells me that God really understands how difficult it is to forgive the unforgivable.

Did you see the motion picture *Forrest Gump*? His lifelong friend, Jenny, was dirt poor. Raised in a dilapidated farmhouse by an alcoholic father, she was physically and sexually abused. Years later, she and Forrest return to her roots. After a few moments of pained silence, Jenny breaks into a rage and hurls handsful of rocks and dirt at the old house. As she falls to the ground weeping uncontrollably, Forrest says calmly, "Sometimes, Jenny, there just aren't enough stones to throw."

Forgiveness is no sweet, platonic ideal to be dispensed to the world like perfume sprayed from a fragrance bottle. It is achingly difficult. Long after you have forgiven, the wound lives on in memory.

PHILIP YANCEY[5]

THE CROSS OF FORGIVENESS

How badly have you been hurt by your loss? How angry are you? How hard is it for you to forgive? You have to start at the cross of Christ. At least this is what the apostle Paul taught the Corinthians. They were having horrific people problems. So he was resolved "to know nothing while I was with you except Jesus Christ and him crucified" (1 Corinthians 2:2).

What does this mean? Every Christian knows that the cross is the only bridge to heaven. There is no other way to be saved, no other way to be reconciled to God the Father, except through the death of his Son on the cross. I think that's pretty clear to most of us, and it's symbolized by the *vertical* beam of the cross.

What isn't so clear is that we need the cross just as much to reconcile our relationships with others, symbolized by the *horizontal* beam of the cross. The cross is about making a way into God's holy presence by bridging the canyon of sin. The cross is also about making a way across the canyon of abuse and offense in our relationships with others.

From the human point of view, there are never enough stones to throw. Forgiveness in some situations is *humanly* impossible. *Forgiveness is an unnatural act.* Indeed, it is so unnatural that the famed Sigmund Freud once wrote, "One must forgive one's enemies, but not before they are hanged."[6]

I and the public know what all schoolchildren learn; those to whom evil is done, do evil in return.

W.H. AUDEN

I own the big, thick (1,223 pages of double columns) *Baker Encyclopedia of Psychology.* Forgiving others, I think, is a huge factor in mental health and personal wholeness, and yet this giant book on human behavior only has a couple of pages on forgiveness. The opening sentence of the brief article on forgiveness, written by J. M. Brandsma, Professor and Director of Clinical Psychology Internship, Department of Psychiatry, Medical College of Georgia (all of those qualifications make his statement especially startling), states: "Even though it has been a continuing problem throughout history, *modern psychological literature does not offer much discussion of the concept of forgiveness.*"[7]

All this has led me to the conclusion that *forgiveness is distinctively Christian.* Not only is the cross the singular way to heaven, it's the only way to heal a broken relationship. It's the only way to heal the past. I need Jesus in me to go to heaven. I need Jesus in me to forgive others. Because forgiveness is an unnatural act—an impossible human act—only possible through the power of God.

> He said to his disciples, "Hard trials and temptations are bound to come, but too bad for whoever brings them on! Better to wear a millstone necklace and take a swim in the deep blue sea than give even one of these dear little ones a hard time!
>
> "Be alert. If you see your friend going wrong, correct him. If he responds, forgive him. Even if it's personal against you and repeated seven times through the day, and seven times he says, 'I'm sorry, I won't do it again,' forgive him."
>
> The apostles came up and said to the Master, **"Give us more faith."** LUKE 17:1-3, *THE MESSAGE*

I take this to mean that forgiving others is impossible without faith, without trust in God to do what we *cannot* do. So if you are having difficulty forgiving…

- Acknowledge your unforgiveness and recognize that it's not just you. *Everyone* wrestles with unforgiveness and yours is no surprise to God.

- Talk to somebody. Ask him or her to pray *with* you now—and *for* you in the weeks and months ahead.

- Pray to God the best you can. Tell him exactly how you feel (he knows anyway), and ask him to remove the unforgiveness. Remember, Jesus, the one who died on the cross so you could be forgiven, is living in you!

- Pray for the person who hurt you, or neglected the person who died, or killed them.

"*Pray* for them?! Are you crazy?"

Was Jesus crazy? No! That's what he told us to do:

> But I tell you who hear me: **Love your enemies, do good to those who hate you, bless those who curse you, pray for those who mistreat you.** If someone strikes you on one cheek, turn to him the other also. If someone takes your cloak, do not stop him from taking your tunic.... Do to others as you would have them do to you.
>
> If you love those who love you what credit is that to you? Even 'sinners' love those who love them. And if you do good to those who are good to you, what credit is that to you? Even 'sinners' do that.... But love your enemies, do good to them.... Then your reward will be great, and you will be sons of the Most High, **because he is kind to the ungrateful and wicked.** Be merciful, just as your Father is merciful. LUKE 6:27-36

An important step to healing your pain and unforgiveness is actually doing good to and praying for the very people who did you wrong.

"Do good to them? *Pray* for them?! How could I ever do that?"

The same way Jesus has been good to you. "He is kind to the ungrateful and wicked." That's you. That's me. Did we deserve it? Not even slightly. In fact, we deserve worse than what we wish on those who have caused us pain. Truman Madsen wrote, "When someone treats you like dirt, you treat them like gold." Like Jesus.

And pray for them. Something powerful happens inside when we begin to pray for those who deserve to be despised. To pray *for* them, not *against* them. It *will not* come easy for you, but you have to believe that God's Word is true, that what Jesus has said in these verses is really in your best interest. "And pray for those who mistreat you."

The alternative is *not* in your best interest:

> Then Peter approached him with the question, "Master, if my brother goes on wronging me how often should I forgive him? Would seven times be enough?"

"No," replied Jesus, "not seven times, but seventy times seven! For the kingdom of Heaven is like a king who decided to settle his accounts with his servants. When he had started calling in his accounts, a man was brought to him who owed him millions of [dollars]. As he had no means of repaying the debt, his master gave orders for him to be sold as a slave, and his wife and children and all his possessions as well, and the money to be paid over. At this the servant fell on his knees before his master, 'Oh, be patient with me!' he cried, 'and I will pay you back every penny!' Then his master was moved with pity for him, set him free and canceled his debt.

"But when this same servant had left his master's presence, he found one of his fellow servants who owed him a few [dollars]. He grabbed him and seized him by the throat, crying, 'Pay up what you owe me!' At this his fellow-servant fell down at his feet, and implored him, 'Oh, be patient with me, and I will pay you back!' But he refused and went out and had him put in prison until he should repay this debt.

"When the other fellow-servants saw what had happened, they were horrified and went and told their master the whole incident. Then his master called him in.

"'You wicked servant!' he said. 'Didn't I cancel all that debt when you begged me to do so? Oughtn't you to have taken pity on your fellow-servant as I, your master, took pity on you?' And his master in anger handed him over to the jailers till he should repay the whole debt. This is how my Heavenly Father will treat you unless you each forgive your brother from the heart."

MATTHEW 8:21-35, PHILLIPS

I realize that the implications of this parable are severe, so severe, in fact, that I hesitated to include it in this book. It's really not a very comforting story, but it does shine a bright light on the terribleness of unforgiveness. If Jesus is telling us anything here, it's that unforgiveness shapes its own private hell.

It's difficult enough to suffer the indignity of insult and the pain of abuse without adding the torment of unresolved unforgiveness.

Pain from others is bad. Unforgiveness just makes it worse, because bitterness is self-destructive. But God wants you healed.

How do you *usually* respond to people who hurt you? Do you *always* go for the jugular? Do you plan revenge *every* time someone treats you badly? Is getting even a way of life? If you *never* even *try* to remove a hateful memory and restore a loving relationship, you are in a lot of trouble.

If you are *trying* to forgive; even if you manage forgiving in fits and starts, if you forgive today, hate again tomorrow, and have to forgive again the day after, you are a forgiver. Most of us are amateurs, bungling duffers sometimes. So what? In this game nobody is an expert. We are all beginners.

LEWIS SMEDES[8]

FORGIVING GOD

Maybe the worst kind of anger is what we feel toward God when it seems like he's responsible for our pain. If God is God, why did he let this terrible thing happen? I know of a man who since his son's accidental death refused to attend church. I don't think he's reading his Bible and praying either. Best-selling author Philip Yancey, who wrote *Disappointment with God*, dedicates his book, "For my brother, who is still disappointed."

Actually, people who unflinchingly blame God probably would not read this book anyway, so if you've gotten this far, it means your heart is open. At least a little. And if you are particularly concerned about how you feel about God, I suggest you jump over to the last chapter, "Unsolved Mysteries," and read that now.

FORGIVING THE PERSON WHO DIED

Right up there with disappointment with God is the terrible frustration of having someone die before you had a chance to heal the hurts between you. Actually, you are probably bouncing back and forth between self-hatred for failing to deal with the problem before the person died, and hating him or her for dying before you had that chance.

I have a solution. The Bible expressly forbids talking to the dead. But it may be helpful if you go to the grave site and, speaking aloud, get things off your chest. You will have the empty feeling that the dead person is not hearing a single word and that is true. But God has access to them! Why don't you just ask God to pass along a message of your grief and shame over failing to reconcile with the deceased? From what I've heard of heaven ...

He will wipe every tear from their eyes. There will be no more death or mourning or crying or pain, for the old order of things has passed away. REVELATION 21:4

Undoubtedly, you are feeling much worse than the person who died. And I'm sure that being in the presence of God, the one who's gone has gotten over the pain. God probably has already told that person how you feel, since he is able to do above and beyond what we ask or think. But it might really help you to say to God what you wish you'd said before the person died. Talk to God about it right now.

EIGHT

Memories
Making a Plan for the Tough Days

The leaves of memory seemed to make
A mournful rustling in the dark.
HENRY WADSWORTH LONGFELLOW

Three weeks from this Friday our oldest son David is getting married. By the time this book is published, he will be well on his way to his first wedding anniversary. Like most mothers, my wife, Marilyn, will probably cry on both days, but not just because she's sentimental about weddings and first anniversaries.

No, Marilyn will probably cry, at least once, because the incredible joy of a family wedding will remind her that her mother, who died a couple years ago, will not be there to enjoy the day with us.

Dave Murrow, whose teenage son died in a drowning accident, wrote to me:

I can't stop thinking about it. It's always with me. It never leaves. It drifts into the background from time to time, but never far. Like closing the door to a really messy room, the mess is still there, and as soon as you open the door, you are confronted by it again. In a way, *everything* I do is done with Daniel in mind. I think about him when I'm eating. When I travel. When I work. Read. Pray. Go to church. Visit with friends. Plan the future. All the time thinking about him.

And Judy Hawk, who also lost her son, adds:

Just when the times are the happiest, I will stop for a moment and see my two grandsons growing into young men. When I do, I always think of how much I wish Robert were with them, watching them, loving them. I can look at Robert's picture, or remember a special holiday with him. There are always reminders of his place in my life, and those are the times when I weep again for my son.

One of our greatest concerns—even fears—was that people would forget Robert. We were afraid that maybe the day would come when we would forget him, too. So I made a point to tell our family and friends to keep talking about Robert. We found, to our dismay, that friends are reluctant to bring up memories of another person's loved one who has died, but the survivors often want to talk about and keep that person fresh in their memory.

BIRTHDAYS, ANNIVERSARIES, HOLIDAYS, AND OTHER SPECIAL OCCASIONS

Just about anything can trigger the memory of a loved one who is gone, but special days—birthdays, anniversaries, and holidays—are especially painful. And the first year is always the worst. You especially dread Christmas, and if you lost a child, the child's birthday is the most terrible reminder that he's gone.

Debbi Edwards wrote to me:

> One day of the year that always catches me by surprise is Mother's Day. The last Mother's Day we celebrated before Eric's death had been very special for me, the best I'd ever had. I said this even before Eric died. Now that memory and the Mother's Day holiday have become, instead, a remembrance of the loss of my son, who is gone forever.
>
> Although special days are still very difficult for me, I am rediscovering peace—and even some joy has returned to my life. Something seems to be calming the troubled waters of my soul. Thank God I no longer experience panic, and I actually feel a measure of peace when I think about Eric being gone for the rest of my life.
>
> The Lord has answered so many prayers in very special ways. These "personal miracles" help me hold on through the bad days. I also remind myself that I will be with my son again one day. I will make it until then, and we'll celebrate together forever.

There are specific things that can help you cope with the crushing memories of special days, particularly during the first year after the death of your loved one.

- *Plan ahead.* Try not to let the special day take you by surprise. Think through what may have become a birthday or holiday routine, and as you do, think about how each aspect of that day may be emotionally difficult. What would you like to do the same? To do differently?

- If it helps, *do things differently*. For example, you may get especially emotional writing Christmas cards. If you can't bear it, skip the tradition for a year or two. Send everyone a simple newsletter, and ask a friend to help you address the envelopes, or just let everybody know the next year why you didn't send a card. You may even want to work on Christmas Day.

- Generally, *do whatever helps you*. If what you do, however, seems unusual or inappropriate for other members of your family, then you need to talk to them about it. If there are several other people affected by your wishes, you may have to compromise.

- *Realize that anticipating the event is often more significant than the event itself.* You will probably (there are exceptions) find the birthday or the holiday less painful than thinking about them.

Special days to think about as you consider how you are going to manage your emotions are:

Birthday
Anniversary
Father's and Mother's Days
Valentine's Day
Easter
July 4
Thanksgiving
Christmas
New Year's Day
Beginning of a season, or the first day of school
First year anniversary of the death

You may wish to add to this list by writing down a holiday or time of year that you know will be special and emotional:

_____

_____

_____

It's probably best to hear it from an "expert." Margie Dalton wrote:

Some days were more difficult than others. Birthdays and holidays were painful. Memories of past happy times would come flooding in so bittersweetly. In the last hours of every Christmas Day, John and I, breathing a giant sigh of relief, would burst out, "We did it! We survived!"

Somehow we had managed to buy some presents and to have a little fun, to go to church, and even to share a meal with each other and with friends without being overwhelmed by our loss.

It takes years to get over the feeling that *someone is missing.* I used to catch myself thinking, "Who is it that's supposed to be here for Christmas? Who hasn't arrived yet?" A moment later I'd realize I was missing one of my children who wasn't ever coming home for Christmas again.

It was often the little things that caused painful reminders: setting the table for five instead of six; then setting the table for four instead of five. And then there was the challenge of packing up and giving away the children's personal things, dealing with them in responsible ways and not allowing bedrooms to become mausoleums and articles of clothing to become fetishes.

Margie's husband John added his thoughts:

When people have lost a very close loved one, they will often think they are going mad during the twelve months after the death. I suggest that on that first anniversary they gather with friends and celebrate. *They have survived!*

For the Christian, this should be a time to dance before the Lord and proclaim, "His mark is on me! I am saved! I am a unique child of the heavenly Father! In spite of all my fears and complaining, I didn't drown in the deep waters of sorrow and grief!"

And in the end we discover that the loss itself is not the ultimate issue. Instead, it's a matter of going ahead with God.

Personally, I have learned to honor the mystery. I still don't have all the answers, but I have learned to live with and tolerate this lack of closure.

I have learned that faith, trust, and hope are not feeble features of benign passivity, little bits of superficial spirituality smeared on top of the grief. No, faith and trust in God—and hope—are basic. They have become for me a substitute for my grief. Instead of grief, I believe God.

THE LITTLE THINGS YOU REMEMBER

Dave Murrow shares a very different perspective on the memories of holidays and special occasions:

Life is made up of the little things. We have a tendency to remember the "big" events: graduations, marriages, special vacations. Like everyone else, I remember the big things, but I miss the little things the most. If I could just hold Daniel's hand in mine, or hear the sound of his voice, what joy that would bring! We mark our life's progress by big events, but it's the little ones that really have importance.

Memories of the Past... a Bridge to the Future

The depth of your sorrow diminishes slowly and at times imperceptibly.

Your recovering is not an act of disloyalty to the person who has died.

Nor is it achieved by "forgetting" the past.

Pictures and mementos may be tangible reminders of days gone by. Don't try to destroy a beautiful part of your life because remembering it hurts.

As children of today and tomorrow,
we are also children of yesterday.

The past still travels with us
and what it has been makes us
what we are.

But memories are not enough.

You must not become a "slave" to
the past by worshiping at the memorial
shrine that you, yourself, have erected.
You must not think, "Everything's
the same. Nothing has changed."

If you believe that, you are preventing
the building of a bridge to the
future.
You would be living in a world made up
exclusively of memories.

Try to strike that delicate balance
between a yesterday that should
be remembered
and a tomorrow that must be created.

EARL A. GROLLMAN[1]

The following is an excerpt from an article by Tony Martorana, founder and director of Christ's Helpers, which appeared in a recent issue of *Charisma Magazine*.

When Memories Bring Pain

We have colorful memories. Like old photographs, memories can bring back both the wonderful and sad moments of our lives.

But memories typically are more than still shots. Rather, our minds are like film projectors that play our Technicolor "video collections." In good times and in bad, running images are placed within the confines of our minds and left there in storage.

When those memories are retrieved, they can be played back on our internal projectors. They can bring us great joy— or intense pain.

Unfortunately, for many of us the memories that remain the most vivid for the longest periods of time are those involving pain and heartache.

It doesn't have to be that way. According to the Bible, those private collections of past hurt and devastation do not have to be the last words on our lives. In fact, those on whom "the Spirit of the Sovereign Lord" rests, Isaiah says, "will rebuild the ancient ruins and restore the places long devastated; they will renew the ruined cities" (Isaiah 61:1,4, NIV).

"Ancient ruins" brings to mind the image of a once beautiful metropolis now devastated: Brick lies upon brick in a heap, and broken columns totter over skeletons of yesterdays long gone.

For many of us, that's a picture of our lives. At one time, our lives were structured and filled with hope and promise. But now, circumstances have taken a hard turn. Life has become disjointed, and our dreams are the bricks in the heap....

We have a Redeemer who's concerned about our past, our present, and our future. Jesus Christ is the restorer of all that the enemy has destroyed. He wants to rebuild the broken dreams of yesterday—our ancient ruins. He wants to bring healing for the past, joy for today and hope for tomorrow.

Life brings pain. That is inevitable. But misery is optional. We don't have to be crushed under the rubble of the past.

That doesn't mean God will take our painful memories away. On the contrary, He is not in the brainwashing business. But He is in the business of healing pain.

In fact, when we take our pain to the Lord and ask Him for insight, He helps us see a purpose in our suffering so that our once painful experiences can be used to help others come through similar difficulties (see 2 Corinthians 1:3-4).

This type of recovery and rehabilitation is not easy. It takes time and a determined willingness.... But we do it with the Lord's help—and "nothing is impossible with God" (Luke 1:37).

In my thirteen years as a minister, I've had many people share their painful memories with me. In some cases, their pain has seemed so fresh, their devastation so intense that I assume the break-up, the death, or the divorce must have happened recently.

I'm often shocked when they tell me it occurred 10 or 15 years ago! Yet these people are still suffering and still afflicted by the pain.

"Father, how long must they suffer?" I cry out in my spirit.

Perhaps you are asking that question regarding your own pain: "How long, O Lord?"

The fact is, you have a say in the answer! God is willing to start *now*! Are you?

TONY MARTORANA[2]

DREAMS

You will very likely dream of your deceased loved one. In fact, you may even hallucinate, which is perhaps one of the most disturbing experiences for many mourners. One would think this would be relatively rare, but studies have found that hallucinations and lifelike dreams are likely to happen to as many as half of America's bereaved.[3]

My wife Marilyn "saw" her mother shortly after her death. We were away on a family vacation in Oregon, a thousand miles or more away from where her mother had died in southern California. Taking a blissful rest in our room, Marilyn was suddenly awakened by a fleeting but unforgettable vision of her mother's face, glowing with joy in the presence of the Lord. It was so real to Marilyn that tears still come to her eyes when she remembers the moment.

Now as any good student of the Bible knows, God strictly forbids seances and calling on the spirits the dead (Deuteronomy 18:11), and I am pleased to report that my wife had no conversation with her mom! Nor did her mother make any attempt to speak with her, or even make eye contact. And it happened only once.

Yet what my wife experienced is, I believe, a biblical possibility. On the Mount of Transfiguration, Moses and Elijah appeared in the presence of Peter, James, and John conversing with Jesus. It surely wasn't something the disciples were able to conjure up, nor did Moses and Elijah speak with them. But it is quite clear from the text of Scripture that this really was Moses and Elijah talking with Jesus, not just apparitions (see Matthew 17:1-13, Mark 9:2-13, and Luke 9:28-36).

Dreaming about your loved one can be startling at times. You may be trying hard to realize he or she is really dead, and wham, you dream about your loved one, alive and well, the two of you having a good time. *Dreaming about the deceased is normal,* sometimes pleasant and sometimes unpleasant. You may not have such dreams, though you may want to. I am a big dreamer and dream almost every night, but it was years before I ever had a dream about my first husband after his death.

Many of the dreams people tell me about are pleasant. Parents often dream of their children at a younger age: a safer time in their lives. Some dream of a loved one appearing to them to let them know that he or she is all right and in a better place. But sometimes dreams are anything but pleasant. Especially after a violent death, the dreamer may be trying vainly to get somewhere or do something to save the loved one. These dreams are very unsettling, making it hard to get back to sleep.

HELEN FITZGERALD[4]

Ultimately, we need the Lord Jesus to help us find healing and resolve. Kristina Buckley, who lost her teenage son in the summer of 1992, wrote to me:

My sixteen-year-old son Matt had only been gone a couple months when Sharon said she wanted to talk to me. She had lost a child and understood my pain. Sharon also knew that Matt had been the type of child who gives his mother a lot of love. That was true. Matt had always gone out of his way to express his love to me, from calling, "I love you, Mom," across a crowded room of adults, to holding my hand at the store. As a teenager he would often call me from a classroom at school just to say, "I love you." One of the hardest things for me to accept was knowing I would not hear those words again.

During our conversation, Sharon hesitantly mentioned to me a time when she felt very close to her daughter. Her daughter had been dead for a while, and yet once when she was sitting in her backyard, she felt suddenly very near her child. The backyard was a favorite place for the two of them, and at this particular time she felt as if her child were there with her again. Sharon reassured me that she didn't see or hear anything. There wasn't anything "weird" about it either. She was just flooded with peace and happiness at the prospect of once again feeling a closeness with her daughter.

I wondered if the Lord would allow me to have a similar experience with Matt. I was not going to go searching for it, but I knew I didn't know enough about what my friend Sharon experienced to judge it as wrong or evil.

Four months later I was at the supermarket looking at special Christmas cards for the holidays. On the bottom shelf, a card with a 1948 Norman Rockwell painting stood out to me. I bent down to read it. The cover said, "Home Is Where Memories Live." Rockwell named his painting "Homecoming," because you can see the smiling faces of family as they greeted a tall, skinny young man.

His mother was hugging him, and under his arms bulged several presents and a leather suitcase that had personal items hanging out. Looking at the smile on the mother's face, I was flooded with a warm peace, reliving a similar joy. With tears in my eyes I opened the card and read,

> *Sometimes I feel like I had to leave home*
> *before I could appreciate my wonderful family.*
> *I miss being able to spend time with you.*
> *I miss you.*

God could not have orchestrated a more lovely, more powerful, more comforting gift to me. I don't think that Matt was there with me, or that he arranged for this to happen to me. I do know that God knew my hurting heart, and in an attempt to comfort and bless me, he allowed me to "feel" especially close to my son once more.

That was the only time I ever felt that type of closeness to Matt since the day he died. I treasure that day.

Memories. Precious memories. And finally, from the Bible, some of the most precious things of all for us to remember...

> Praise the Lord, O my soul;
> all my inmost being, praise his holy name.
> Praise the Lord, O my soul,
> **and forget not all his benefits—**
> who forgives all your sins
> and heals all your diseases,
> who redeems your life from the pit
> and crowns you with love and compassion,
> who satisfies your desires with good things
> so that your youth is renewed like
> the eagle's. PSALMS 103:1-5

> Look to the Lord and his strength;
> seek his face always.
> **Remember the wonders he has done,**
> his miracles, and the judgments

he pronounced,
O descendants of Israel his servant,
O sons of Jacob, his chosen ones.
1 CHRONICLES 16:11-13

And some things to forget...

Not that I have already obtained all this, or have already been made perfect, but I press on to take hold of that for which Christ Jesus took hold of me. Brothers, I do not consider myself yet to have taken hold of it. But one thing I do: **Forgetting what is behind and straining toward what is ahead**, I press on toward the goal to win the prize for which God has called me heavenward in Christ Jesus. PHILIPPIANS 3:12-14

NINE

Saying Good-Bye
Bringing Closure to Your Grief

It is only the souls that do not love that go empty
in this world.

ROBERT HUGH BENSON

Yesterday afternoon there were three slightly frantic messages on my answering machine. All were from the same family. They were trying to phone me from a local mortuary where they had gone to make final arrangements for the funeral of their mother.

After several return calls, I was finally able to reach them at the home of their parents. "My father would be so blessed if you could do the service, but he's in no shape to come to the phone right now," his son informed me. "He and mom were married for fifty-seven years, and he's taking this really hard."

"Fifty-seven years!" I echoed loudly. I knew the couple was elderly, and that they had been married only to one another, but when I heard specifically how long they had been together, it made a special impression.

"It's so difficult to say good-bye," I thought to myself. And the better you know someone—the closer you are to another—the *more* difficult it is.

SAYING HELLO MEANS THAT SOMEDAY YOU HAVE TO SAY GOOD-BYE

"Now I commit you to God and to the word of his grace, which can build you up and give you an inheritance among all those who are sanctified.... In everything I did, I showed you that by this kind of hard work we must help the weak, remembering the words the Lord Jesus himself said: 'It is more blessed to give than to receive.'"

When he had said this, he knelt down with all of them and prayed. **They all wept** as they embraced him and kissed him. **What grieved them most was his statement that they would never see his face again.** Then they accompanied him to the ship. ACTS 20:32-38

If the Ephesian Christians had never said hello to the apostle Paul, in the sense that they received him into their lives, they would never have had to say good-bye. They would never have been grieved to see him go. If they had never loved, they never would have cried.

138

Grief means simply that there was once someone special in your life, and now that special person is gone.

My wife's dad has lived on the same sunny little southern California citrus farm since 1939. A long and narrow sloping driveway curls through the orange grove, past their rose garden, and onto the shady lawn of their cozy farmhouse—our favorite family destination every summer and nearly every Christmas.

After two weeks of San Diego attractions and Mom's great meals, our small children were only sad that they were in for a long, boring drive through the endless desert back to Phoenix. But I can still see Grandma and Grandpa standing on that front lawn as they watched the shrinking taillights of our car. Waving good-bye. Fighting back tears.

Actually, I didn't fully realize how difficult those farewells were for them until just last week, when our newly married son and daughter-in-law rolled their overloaded Ryder moving truck out of our driveway and into a new life in California.

I get weepy writing about it.

It's so hard to say good-bye.

If I never loved, I never would have cried.

And they're not even going away *forever.*

Good Night, Sandy

Leighton Ford, an associate evangelist with Billy Graham for many years, wrote about the death of his son Sandy and an imaginary conversation he had with him:

During the months following Sandy's death, to cope with my grief and sense of loss I kept a journal. Through a series of "conversations" with Sandy, I continued to express my grief and bring our relationship to a close.

In one of those chats, I said, "Sandy, you've been dead two months earthtime."

"I feel as if I have been alive forever, Dad. It's a lot like one big long today."

"It's not a matter of time, Sandy, except that time heals. It's more a matter of nearness. I guess I'm concerned that as our time goes on, we will lose any sense of nearness."

"But why, Dad? You're moving closer to eternity every day. You're no longer moving from, but to me! And besides, the 'Wall' between is so thin—you would laugh if you could see it."

"I think more of you than when you were at Chapel Hill."

"Sure! I know you do. I hear those thoughts."

"Night, son! Enjoy the stars!"

"It's morning here, Dad. Enjoy the light!"[1]

"Good-Bye" Is Not Forever

For the Christian, it's "good-bye for now."

Yes, I know it still hurts a lot, even if you know you will see your loved one again in heaven. It hurts because there were so many things you wanted to do together here on earth. Like just hold each other once more. But believing that one day we will come together again in the presence of the Lord—just knowing that—dulls the pain, even if ever so slightly.

> Brothers, we do not want you to be ignorant about those who fall asleep, **or to grieve like the rest of men, who have no hope.** We believe that Jesus died and rose again and so we believe that God will bring with Jesus those who have fallen asleep in him. According to the Lord's own word, we tell you that we who are still alive, who are left till the coming of the Lord, will certainly not precede those who have fallen asleep. For the Lord himself will come down from heaven with a loud command, with the voice of the archangel and with the trumpet call of God, and the dead in Christ will rise first. After that, we who are still alive and are left will be caught up together **with them** in the clouds to meet the Lord in the air. And so we will be with the Lord forever. **Therefore encourage each other with these words.** 1 Thessalonians 4:13-18

How Do You Say Good-bye?

How can you say good-bye when someone you love dies without saying good-bye to you? I don't have statistics to prove it, but it seems that most people who die don't have a chance to say good-bye to the ones they love. And certainly those who love the ones who die don't get to say good-bye either.

My wife's mother passed away unexpectedly in her sleep. She wasn't very healthy—diabetes and a weak heart—but no one in the family had any notion that the little nap she took before dinner one summer evening would last forever.

So how do you say good-bye? For my wife, it's been a long process. Saying good-bye is really about everything in the grief process. Yet there are specific things we can do to help bring closure.

This week I heard a radio news report of a family in Utah whose teenage son fell to his death exploring an abandoned mine. Because of the aging, unstable mine shaft, the professional rescue team called off the search, but the family persisted. In what was termed a small miracle, members of the boy's family recovered his body—just so they could bring closure. Just so he could have a "decent burial." Just so they could say good-bye.

Seeing the body. Touching the body. Burying or cremating the body. A funeral, then, is the first formal step in saying good-bye.

But it takes more than that, especially if there is no body, or if the body is so mangled or decomposed that seeing the one you love one more time is impossible.

Visiting the Grave

Debbi Edwards graciously agreed to share her feelings with me and with you about saying good-bye to her murdered son. I asked her specifically to write about "saying good-bye"—what she felt and what she did.

One of the most difficult days was the one when Eric was buried. Because Eric's body had been in the desert for two weeks, its decomposition made it impossible for me to see my son one last time to say good-bye. I have since read that seeing the body is important for closure. I am quite sure that, because of this, it has been more difficult for me to accept Eric's death.

When the graveside service was over, I found I was unable to leave. I finally asked to be alone with my son. Part of me wanted to scream and run, while everything else in me wanted desperately to open the casket, but I knew I couldn't. So instead, I gently stroked his casket and quietly walked away.

Following the service, I found myself drawn to Eric's graveside daily. I wouldn't stay long, but I hardly missed a day for the first three or four months following his death. I found myself standing beside Eric's grave. Sometimes I rearranged the flowers. Sometimes I cleaned the grave marker. Sometimes I prayed. I was always trying to find a little more comfort and release in saying good-bye and letting go.

Over the last four years the visits to Eric's resting place have become less frequent, although I still feel drawn there on the anniversary of his death and on his birthday. I take flowers and, standing over his grave, I feel the terrible pain of his absence in our family.

WRITING A LETTER

There is no magic formula. Different people have different ways of saying good-bye. Gwen Ellis, who works for Servant/Vine Books and who competently edited this book, agreed to share her own story of loss, and how she said good-bye to her little twins:

I was six months pregnant and really hadn't been feeling too well, but I kept going. Kept going, that is, until one Sunday morning at the end of March when I stepped out of bed and realized my water had broken and the birth of this too-soon baby was imminent. What I did not know until I was X-rayed at the hospital a short time later was that I carried twins. Oh, how I had always wanted twins! Now they were on the way, and it was too early.

My little girls were born at 10:30 Sunday morning and finished their visit to earth at 6 P.M. that same day. Suddenly we were plunged into grief. But there was a problem I did not become aware of until many years later. My husband had been through some very great traumas in his life. His last look at his own father was of him pleading soundlessly from a hospital bed, begging with his eyes to be released. I was young and did not understand the significance of this event upon my husband's ability to grieve. I was left to grieve on my own and didn't do it very well. He seemed to be taking it in stride and I was crushed. I felt there was something wrong with me that I was so torn up by their deaths.

Time wore on, and many years later I found myself in counseling, trying to sort out this tragedy along with many other events in my life. I told my counselor about my loss and he asked about when I'd said good-bye to my babies. I couldn't tell him. It had been decided that I was probably too weak to go to their funeral, so I hadn't even been able to say good-bye to them. It was several months before I finally saw their grave.

The counselor said, "Gwen, it is my experience that if you cannot tell me the time and place, you probably haven't done it, and you cannot finish your grief until you say good-bye."

He suggested I write them a letter, telling them all the longing of my heart where they were concerned; telling them of my love; telling them I was looking forward to getting to know them in heaven. He assured me I might feel that it was a useless, time-wasting act, but to do it anyway.

I went home and wrote and wrote and wrote. I wrote all the agony, passions, and loneliness I felt for the girls. Then I sealed the letter and put it in a safe place. I have never looked at it again. I have not needed to do so. But an interesting thing has happened. For many years I experienced phantom grief. I don't know if that's a psychological term, but what happened was that I would not be thinking about the twins and then all of a sudden I would dream about them or think about them all day long.

Then, when I looked at the calendar, I'd see that it was their birthday. After I wrote the letter, all of that disappeared. It has never happened again to this day.

Please don't think me crass, but I had two dogs—a miniature poodle and a golden cocker spaniel. The poodle was my dog for fourteen years, and one night she got in the way of a truck and was badly injured. I picked her up and took her to the vet to be put down. The cocker was my son's dog, but after he left home she came to live with me. She was very ill and I could no longer care for her. When she was ten years old and still very beautiful, I had to put her down, too.

I grieved their loss, but not very openly. After all, they were just dogs. But they'd each been at my side constantly throughout their whole lives and I felt a terrible loss. After writing the letter to the twins, who had never lived with me, I wrote a letter to each of my pets and said good-bye. I put those letters away also, and somehow the process ended my grief for them as well.

It's a simple idea. Write and say good-bye to the one who left you behind. It works.

TOUCHING THE PAST

Debbi Edwards shared another unique experience of closure:

Eric's car was very special. He and his dad had spent two years building the car, complete with a custom paint job and intricate graphics. One of the young men who murdered our son had driven the car from Arizona to California, where it was found torched.

Some time later, I was desperately seeking points of closure to Eric's death, and I had this strong feeling that I needed to see his car. After being informed by the local police department that there was no reason to bring the vehicle back to Arizona, a friend of mine offered to fly with me to California to view Eric's car.

No sooner had I begun to make arrangements than a local police detective let us know the car had been brought back to Arizona after all. Within a couple of days, I was at the impound yard with my friend, looking at the car.

My son had died in that car.

There wasn't much left, except for one small spot on the lower part of the front fender. For some reason, it was untouched by the fire. The special paint and graphics that meant so much to Eric were still intact!

Weeping, I tenderly touched that very spot. It really helped me.

Remembering

Sometimes the person who died gives us subtle indications *before* they die, and we wonder if we are imagining it. Several people who have shared their insights for this book have told me about little incidents that, now, looking back, give them the assurance their loved one was somehow saying good-bye. "In the wake of our son's death," Kristina Buckley told me, "I have been reminded again and again of the place in the Bible that tells us our days are numbered (Daniel 5:26), that God knows exactly how long we are going to live and he has determined that in advance. If that's true, then there is every reason for me to believe that he will let us know, perhaps even through the one who is about to die, that it's time to say good-bye."

Dave Murrow, who lost his son and who also happens to be Kristina's neighbor, wrote to me:

On the twenty-sixth day of Dan's coma, when his mom and I entered his room, he turned his head and "looked" at us. First at me, then at his mother. He didn't smile, but his face seemed animated. He "communicated" with us, we are sure, "in the spirit," when it was impossible for him to do so "in the flesh." He was literally blind, in a coma, and nearly dead, but spiritually he was alive. And in that spirit, he "spoke" to us.

I had never experienced such a thing with another human being. I'm not even sure what Dan was communicating. A message of love? Or perhaps a good-bye? A closure? He seemed so peaceful after that moment, and the very next morning he died.

I wish I knew more about what we "said" to each other, what God was trying to accomplish through that exchange, but I don't. I think about it often, though, wishing I could reverse time and relive it, stretch it out, prolong the moment, or even record it on video, but I can't. For weeks we dialogued with doctors, nurses, family, and friends. So many words, most of which we don't remember. Then, in a sliver of time, we "spoke" with Daniel. Little things like that mean so much.

PRAYER

Paul Edwards, Debbi's husband, wrote the following letter for Eric less than a month after Eric was murdered. I am so grateful that Paul was willing to share this very personal moment with you. He hopes and prays that some good thing, however small, might come out of his unspeakable suffering.

December 21, 1991

Dear Jesus,

I don't know if Eric can see or hear me, so I ask if you would please read this to him for me.

Son, I love you. I had a wrong attitude toward you the last months of your life. How I wish now I could have held you in my arms. In my mind I have even pictured myself kissing you on the forehead. I want to do that when I see you again. Okay?

I never knew how much I loved you until now. I am going to miss you so much. I wish we could have gone out to the park-n-swap to look at speakers for my car. Remember, I asked if you would help me install a stereo system? You really wanted to, and told me what would work the best in the Volkswagen.

Eric, a lot of people have said real good things about you. I hurt inside right now to think I was so self-centered. I can hardly believe that all I wanted was for you to move out of our house and try to make it on your own. It was only because I didn't want any more hassles. I'd take all those hassles back right now if it meant I could see you again. I really would.

We had some good times, didn't we? Remember that hunting trip, when I had to rest your rifle on my shoulder 'cause you couldn't even hold it up. Ha, ha! And remember the other time we were hunting, when we fooled Carl and his dad with raisins, making them think it was deer droppings?! Good one, huh?

We had some bad times too, and I can't forget them either, but I want to remember the good ones. Okay? You touched a lot of people, especially my life now that I see and understand things more clearly. I wish you weren't gone—so I could start over again. I really hoped God was going to give me a second chance, but that didn't happen, and I don't know why. I am sure you do, now that you are in God's presence. I pray that someday God will show me too.

I love you, Eric, with all my heart, soul, and being. Good-bye, Eric, till I come to be with you in heaven.

Love, Dad

PART TWO

SUFFERING

Understanding
God

TEN

Sin and Death
What Happens to Us When We Die?

The summons of death comes to us all, and no one can die for another. Everyone must fight his own battle with death by himself alone.

MARTIN LUTHER

Not only do we know God through Jesus Christ, but we only know ourselves through Jesus Christ. Apart from Jesus Christ we cannot know the meining of our life or death, or God or of ourselves.

PASCAL

There is a time for everything, and a season for every activity under heaven: a time to be born and a time to die.

ECCLESIASTES 3:1-2

What is death and what's it like to die? No one living knows for sure. I can't tell you. I've never died, and when I do I won't be writing any more books. "Dying is like—nothing on earth," writes Michael Simpson. "The nature of death is uncertain, for, by definition, the dead do not return to tell us what it is like."[1]

And yet, maybe there is more about death for us to know than we think. A lot of our ignorance is self-imposed (we don't want to think about it) and cultural (people around us don't want to talk about it) and spiritual (we don't know as much about the Bible as we should).

Just a hundred years ago, in most of the Western world, life expectancy was a mere thirty-four years. "But today it has doubled," writes theologian Hans Küng. "This means," he explains, "that formerly every child came into contact with death as a matter of course, with that of his sisters or brothers, parents, grandparents. Today only a very few children have seen the corpse of a relative."[2]

My mother, for example, remembers the bodies of family members resting in peace in the parlor of their Michigan farmhouse. But today, about the only thing kids know about dying is what they see on TV or in the movies. In our culture, death is sterile. People die in institutions, covered bodies in windowless vans are transported to mortuaries, and often the remains are cremated or sealed in a casket, never to be seen by the family. It's as if Uncle Harry just vanished into thin air.

What in the Middle Ages was known as the *ars morendi*, the 'art of dying,' is something for which our society has not developed any sort of cultural background.

HANS KÜNG[3]

We can't fully penetrate the veil of mystery that enshrouds human death, but perhaps by thoughtful reflection we can recover something of the "art of dying." This should be especially true for Christians, who are supposed to have the "right" attitude about death.

What Is Death?

Clinical death is when the heart stops beating, blood pressure is unreadable, and the body temperature drops. It is generally agreed that a patient is dead when the vital functions utterly fail.

Sure death is the total absence of brainwave activity. A committee of physicians, lawyers, theologians, and scientists at Harvard determined what was to be considered "brain death." Four criteria were listed:

1. Unreceptivity and unresponsivity
2. No movements or breathing
3. No reflexes
4. Flat electroencephalogram

The most complete definition of death seems to be "an irreversible loss of the vital functions." Death, then, is defined as the state in which physical resuscitation is impossible....

To the materialistic thinker, death means complete annihilation. For the Hindu and the Buddhist, death means reincarnation. To the terrorist, death provides a way to be rewarded for his cause....

Today, the whole question of "when is a person dead" is being discussed more ardently than at any other time in recent history. A relatively new discipline called thanatology (from the Greek *thanatos*, or death) has entered our language and classrooms. Thanatology is the study, or science, of death.

Making his investigation of death and dying in America today, David Dempsey wrote that "our society has secularized life. In so doing it has removed death from its traditional religious context, the belief that it is part of the natural order of things. When death was viewed more theologically, when suffering itself was thought of as spiritually purifying, when men believed in some kind of afterlife that justified suffering, death was more acceptable."

....The Bible tells us precisely what death is. Physical death is separation of the spirit and soul from the body: "...the body without the spirit is dead" (James 2:26). But there is a far worse death, and that is spiritual death. Spiritual death is separation from God.

BILLY GRAHAM[4]

Can you say the word dead?
Try.
Death is a fact, a bitter fact.
Face it.

EARL A. GROLLMAN[5]

The hardest subject in the world, the tears and groans of mankind.

SHELDON VANAUKEN

All we have to do is live long enough, and we will be bereaved. All we have to do is live long enough, and we will die.

D.A. CARSON[6]

In the spirit I rejoice, but my flesh is sorrowful. The flesh doesn't accept this very readily. This separation troubles me very much. It is a strange thing to grieve so much even though I know that she is at peace and very well off.

MARTIN LUTHER,
ON THE DEATH OF HIS DAUGHTER

My grandfather died and then my grandmother died because she wanted to be with my grandfather because they were married for fifty years and they like to play cards.

A CHILD'S VIEW OF DEATH[7]

WHAT IS IT LIKE TO DIE?

From a clinical perspective, death is the cessation of life. Although the cause of death—an accident or illness—certainly may be traumatic, I have not read anywhere that the actual, final experience of death is painful or even unpleasant. In fact, for many people who are suffering from a terminal illness, death is a time of release and peace for both them and their immediate families. "Precious in the sight of the Lord," declares the psalmist, "is the death of his saints" (Psalms 116:15).

For thousands of years, the hard side of death has been softened by describing the dead person as merely "sleeping" or "forgetting." But these terms say, in effect, that "death is simply the annihilation of conscious experience, forever."[8] This is what makes death so terrifying for so many people. "Forgetting" may mean the end of all bad memories, but death means the end of all good memories, too. Sleeping may be the pleasurable end of a tiring day, but death means you're never waking up to another cup of hot coffee.

Is there more? Yes! The Bible describes death as a transition, a passing from one dimension to another, from time and space into eternity. In the parable of the rich man and Lazarus the beggar, Jesus noted that the "time came when the beggar died and the angels carried him to Abraham's side."[9] Simple. Later, when Jesus was dying alongside another criminal, he reassured him, "I tell you the truth, today you will be with me in paradise."[10] Not surprisingly, the apostle Paul held the same view:

I eagerly expect and hope that I will in no way be ashamed, but will have sufficient courage so that now as always Christ will be exalted in my body, whether by life or by death. For to me, to live is Christ and to die is gain. If I am to go on living in the body, this will mean fruitful labor for me. Yet what shall I choose? I do not know! I am torn between the two: I desire to depart and be with Christ, which is better by far; but it is more necessary for you that I remain in the body. PHILIPPIANS 1:20-24

For the Christian, to die is to be with Jesus in paradise the very day your life ends. To say it another way, death is the end of one life and the beginning of another. "In my end is my beginning," wrote the poet T. S. Eliot. Physician and author Diane Komp calls death "a window to heaven," which is the title of her wonderful book about children and death.[11]

What! A wonderful book about children dying? Losing a child is not even *slightly* wonderful, but Dr. Komp decided to study carefully *how* children die. What she found was so startling, and so wonderful, that she became a Christian.

Children Tell Us What It's Like to Die

Since I first began publicly to tell these children's remarkable stories, some have linked my work with what has been described as the "near-death" experience. Although the reported near-death experiences bear some superficial similarities to some aspects of these stories of children who would soon die, there are also striking differences.

Most near-death stories involve adults who are afraid to tell their experiences to anyone for fear that they will not be believed. The young children who experience these visions, however, never question that they will be believed. Unlike the adults whom they tell, the children share their stories without a trace of reticence.

If I could use one word to summarize the adult experiences it would be *Aha!* A more apropos summary word for the children would be *Amen.*

For adults, the experience is often spiritually *revolutionary*, a type of conversion experience that puts them on a new road. For children, however, the experience is more spiritually *evolutionary*, progress on an already familiar pathway.

The adults frequently report vague spiritual beginnings, but the children are more specific, naming Jesus or describing angels....

Young children sick with advanced cancer are similar to adults in reporting peaceful feelings or seeing light. I have never heard a young child suffering from cancer report seeing a tunnel or darkness, feeling they were "out-of-body," or having a review of life events. These are common components of near-death experiences in adults.

Many of the reports from adults take place in the setting of clinical death, coma, or another form of brain impairment. The children I am describing report experiences in dreams, visions, or prayer and are infrequently brain dysfunctional at the time.

DIANE KOMP[12]

WHY DO PEOPLE DIE?

Perhaps a more difficult question than "What's it like to die?" is, "Why do people die?" The simple answer: accidents, illness, and old age. But we all know that death is a deeper issue than what's in the coroner's report. To me, the enormous fascination all of us have with death, coupled with our disbelief and denial any time someone close to us dies, is living proof that human beings are not really supposed to die.

Even the way human societies prepare their dead for burial or cremation—the way we say our good-byes—tells me that there's something immortal inside mortals. Something about us is subject to death. Something else isn't.

This is part of what theologians call "natural revelation," an innate sense of God and eternal things without the benefit of the

Bible. "For since the creation of the world," the apostle Paul attests, "God's invisible qualities—his eternal power and divine nature—have been clearly seen, being understood from what has been made, so that men are without excuse" (Romans 1:20).

As I said in an earlier chapter, people are so God-sensitive at funerals because death arouses our spiritual nature. It's a reminder that we were created in the image of God, that we were intended to live forever, and—*oh, how people hate to admit it*— that we are sinful. And that's really why people die. The experience of death is a dreadful self-disclosure, a grinding collision between who we really are and a God who expects of us much more than we could ever be.

... like the experience of Antonio Parr in Frederick Buechner's *Open Heart*. As he stood at the Brooklyn graveside of his twin sister, "something stirring in the air or quick movement of squirrel or bird brought me back to myself," Parr recounts, "and just at the instant... I knew that the self I'd been brought back to was some fine day going to be as dead as Miriam... Through grace alone I banged right into it—not a lesson this time, a collision."

TIMOTHY K. JONES[13]

Clinically, death is the end of physical life. Biblically, death is the terrible consequence of human sin. The Bible goes so far as to call it a curse. But the Word of God also tells us about Jesus, God's Son, who came to die for the sins of the world, to rise from the dead, and to release us from the grip of death.

Sin entered the world through one man, and death through sin, and in this way death came to all men... ROMANS 5:12

The wages of sin is death, but the gift of God is eternal life in Christ Jesus our Lord. ROMANS 6:23

Just as man is destined to die once, and after that to face judgment, so Christ was sacrificed once to take away the sins of many people; and he will appear a second time, not to bear sin, but to bring salvation to those who are waiting for him. HEBREWS 9:27-28

Jesus said to her, "I am the resurrection and the life. He who believes in me will live, even though he dies; and whoever lives and believes in me will never die. **Do you believe this?**"

"Yes, Lord," she told him, "I believe that you are the Christ, the Son of God, who was to come into the world." JOHN 11:25-26

We can't get around death, and we have no hope of saving ourselves. But Jesus can. Knowing Christ doesn't make death go away, but it takes away the fear of death. Knowing Christ does not take away the sorrow of death, but it takes away the finality and hopelessness of death. *"Do you believe this?"*

What's Gonna Happen to Us?

Do you remember that wonderful chapter in *Bambi* in which no one appears except the dried leaves still clinging to the oak tree long after the others had fallen?

They were silent for a while. Then the first leaf said quietly to herself, "Why must we fall?"

The second leaf asked, "What happens to us when we have fallen?"

"We sink down..."

"What is under us?"

The first leaf answered, "I don't know, some say one thing, some another, but nobody knows."

The second leaf asked, "Do we feel anything, do we know anything about ourselves when we're down there?"

The first leaf answered, "Who knows? Not one of all those down there has ever come back to tell us about it."[14]

I think those lines take us about as far as human reason can manage. And as we read on in the chapter, we find that one of the leaves has learned to welcome life as it is, while the other has not. Each sees part of the truth, each has a certain dignity.

But you and I believe that one of those who fell down has come back to tell us about it. Tell us what? Not that there's nothing to fear, not that we should simply welcome death. Not, however, that we should simply oppose it forever, since he did not, and we follow after him. Maybe Reynold Price's phrase wasn't too bad: When the time has clearly come, we give death a "dignified nod." It's a great evil, but we trust that God can make something good of it—for us, as for Jesus. That takes us [a lot] farther than the leaves could see.

―――――

"Let's remember how beautiful it was, how wonderful, when the sun came out and shone so warmly that we thought we'd burst with life. Do you remember? And the morning dew, the mild and splendid nights...."

A moist wind blew, cold and hostile, through the tree-tops.

"Ah, now," said the second leaf. "I..." Then her voice broke off. She was torn from her place and spun down.

Winter had come.

―――――

Some magnificent beauties, then the coming of that cold and hostile wind. Apart from Jesus, I think that's pretty much the truth of life.

ANONYMOUS, "LETTERS TO A DAUGHTER"[15]

The Christian view of death	The secular view of death
Death is unnatural.	Death is natural.
Death is the result of sin.	Death is just a part of life.
Death is a time of sorrow.	Death is a time of despair.
Death will die when Christ returns.	Death will always be there.

All the humanistic concepts about death being "natural" or part of human nature are false. Death tears man in half. Man was made to live, not die.

ROBERT MOREY[16]

How you understand death will have a huge impact on how you live. Jesus made this very clear in his parable of the prosperous man.

And he told them this parable: "The ground of a certain rich man produced a good crop. He thought to himself, 'What shall I do? I have no place to store my crops.'

"Then he said, 'This is what I'll do. I will tear down my barns and build bigger ones, and there I will store all my grain and my goods. And I'll say to myself, "You have plenty of good things laid up for many years. Take life easy; eat, drink and be merry."'

"But God said to him, 'You fool! This very night your life will be demanded from you. Then who will get what you have prepared for yourself?'" LUKE 12:16-20

When life is easy, it's easy to forget that it won't last forever. That it might not last the night. Death is a sudden, terrible reminder that there are some things in life more important than others.

Awareness of death, and of its opening to a life beyond, has not only framed how I look at life. It has also begun to work a change in how I walk through life. It has, in other words, brought not just new meaning to my moments, but changes my behavior. As Samuel Johnson reportedly said, "When a man knows he is going to be hanged in two weeks, it concentrates his mind wonderfully." Our awareness of the transitoriness of this life, I find, concentrates my priorities, helps me fashion my daily chores.

TIMOTHY K. JONES[17]

Adieu, farewell earth's bliss,
This world uncertain is;
Fond are life's lustful joys,
Death proves them all but toys,
None from his darts can fly.
I am sick, I must die.
Lord, have mercy on us!

Haste, therefore, each degree,
To welcome destiny.
Heaven is our heritage,
Earth but a player's stage;
Mount we unto the sky.
I am sick, I must die.
Lord, have mercy on us!

THOMAS NASH (1567-1601)

SEVEN THINGS YOU SHOULD KNOW ABOUT NEAR-DEATH EXPERIENCES (NDEs)

May 29, 1969, during a firefight in Vietnam, Capt. Tommy Clack was hit in the right foot by an explosive. "I was immediately thrown in the air, and when I landed on the ground, I sat up and realized that my legs, my right arm and my right shoulder were gone. I lay down thinking I would die. I then lost my vision, but I was aware that medics were trying to save me. All of a sudden I was out of my body, looking at them working on me, and then they covered me with a poncho, indicative of death. We arrived at a MASH unit, and I was taken into an operating room. I watched them cut off my uniform, and at this point a massive bright light permeated the room. It was a wonderful, warm, good thing, like looking into the sun. Then, in a blink, I was back out at the battlefield. Around me were people I had served with who had died. They were moving away from me, communicating not with words. They were not in physical form, but I knew that was Dallas, Ralph, Terry, and they knew me. They tried to get me to go with them, but I would not go. Then, in the blink of an eye, I was back in the operating room, watching the scenario."[18]

This is a typical description of a "near-death experience," or "NDE." Numbers of people have "died," only to be resuscitated, and many of those, like Tommy Clack, have been able to describe the unusual events accompanying their "death." What do we know about NDEs and what do they mean?

First, *NDEs are a surprisingly common experience with many similar elements.* Based on his interviews with over a hundred subjects, physician and best-selling author Raymond A. Moody has developed a composite description of a typical NDE:

> A man is dying and, as he reaches the point of greatest physical distress, he hears himself pronounced dead by his doctor. He begins to hear an uncomfortable noise, a loud ringing or buzzing, and at the same time feels himself moving very rapidly through a long, dark tunnel. After this, he finds himself outside of his own physical body.... Soon, other things begin to happen. Others come to meet and help him. He glimpses the spirits of relatives and friends who have already died, and a loving, warm spirit of a kind he has never encountered before—*a being of light*—appears before him.[19]

According to a recent article in *Life* magazine, pollsters estimate that about eight million Americans have had near death experiences![20]

Second, *NDEs are also common among children,* with elements similar to but less corrupted and diverse than the experiences of adults, according to physician Melvin Morse, author of *Closer to the Light: Learning from the Near-Death Experiences of Children.*[21]

Third, something that may be unsettling to Christians, *NDEs are not necessarily related to a person's religious orientation.* In his book *Adventures in Immortality*, the famed pollster George Gallup, who is also a professing Christian, observed "that those with Christian content in their [NDEs] constitute a minority of those responding...

[An NDEs is] as likely to happen to those with little or no religious orientation as it is to those who are very religious."[22]

Fourth, Dr. Moody found that *NDEs have a life-changing impact on the people who have had them*.[23] A few years ago, a young woman in our church shared with me about her brush with death in a car wreck. She had an NDE much like those described in *Life After Life,* and she told me with a reverent hush, "It radically changed my life." As a result, she made a significant recommitment of her life to Christ.

Fifth, *NDEs have a profound effect on the researchers.* Oncologist and professor of pediatrics at Yale University, Diane Komp, whom we met earlier in this chapter, confessed to *Life* magazine, "When I was in medical school, I was hanging out somewhere on the nebulous continuum between agnostic and atheist."[24] But now, in her book *A Window to Heaven*, she writes openly of her faith in Jesus.

Sixth, *NDEs are implied in the Bible.* Paul, it seems, had an out-of-the-body experience, which some Bible scholars believe occurred when he was stoned in Lystra (Acts 14:19-20). He later wrote to the Corinthians,

> I know a man in Christ [Paul himself] who fourteen years ago was caught up to the third heaven. Whether it was in the body or out of the body I do not know—God knows. And I know that this man—whether in the body or apart from the body I do not know, but God knows—was caught up to paradise. He heard inexpressible things, things that man is not permitted to tell.
>
> 2 CORINTHIANS 12:1-4

Seventh, *not every NDE is strictly biblical.* In fact, a recent bestselling book, *Embraced by the Light,* about one woman's phenomenal personal experience in heaven, has been shown to be filled with distinctively Mormon teaching that has no basis in biblical truth. So every NDE must be submitted to the scrutiny and judgment of God's Word.

In summary then,

- People really have these experiences.
- Not all NDEs are positive and pleasant.
- Some research indicates that NDEs can be explained physiologically, although brain researchers haven't come even close to explaining a common feature of NDEs: "the light."[25]
- NDEs tell us little or nothing about who God is and what he expects of us. At best, NDEs are clinical/religious experiences that point to life after death.
- Supernatural phenomena are tricky. They are difficult if not impossible to "prove." Only God's Word is the final authority on death and life after death.
- If NDEs point us to Jesus, great! If they lull us into a false peace about death and dying, especially if we come to the conclusion that everybody in the end is going to heaven, they are a terrible deception.

So that's what happens when you die and come back. In the next chapter we're going to talk about what happens when you die and *don't* come back.

Heaven, Your Real Home
Passing from One Life to a Better One

> Stand we tall together
> for the first time ever
> then fall, please, on grateful knees...
> Eternity is ours.
>
> JONI EARECKSON TADA

If you think talking about death is difficult, try to tell someone what you believe about heaven and hell. Even Christian theologians can't agree fully on precisely what happens when you die. And then there's the maze of popular misconceptions. Have you ever seen a comic strip of some guy sitting on a cloud and strumming a harp? Or have you laughed at Gary Larson's "Far Side" cartoons about hell?

The afterlife has become whatever people want to imagine. But it isn't that way. Although the Bible is not as specific as some might like it to be in the way it presents the subject of life after death, God's Word is quite clear that there is a hell to avoid and a heaven to gain—and that your relationship with God in the here-and-now has everything to do with what happens when you die.

In spite of the risk, I really feel it is necessary in a book on grief to talk about what everyone wonders when someone they love dies. Where did they go? Did they go *anywhere*? Where will *you* go when *you* die? And are there options? Choices?

Death: A Separation of Soul and Body

The Scriptures represent death as primarily a separation of soul and body. "The dust returns to the ground it came from, and the spirit returns to God who gave it," (Ecclesiastes 12:7). Death is a transition from one realm to another, and from one kind of life to another. For the Christian it means the cleansing of the soul from the last vestiges of sin and an entrance into the mansions of light. This is well expressed in the Westminster Shorter Catechism, where, in response to the question, "What benefits do believers receive from Christ at death?" (Q. 37), the answer is given: "The souls of believers are at their death made perfect in holiness, and do immediately pass into glory; and their bodies, being still united to Christ, do rest in their graves, till the resurrection."

LORAINE BOETTNER[1]

When Christians die, their souls go right into the presence of the Lord in heaven. Jesus assured the thief dying on the cross next to him, "*Today* you will be with me in paradise."[2] And the apostle Paul taught that to be absent from the body is to be present with the Lord (see 2 Corinthians 5:6-9).

Yet the Bible, especially the New Testament, also puts a huge emphasis on the resurrection of our physical bodies from the dead, which means there is a time gap between the moment of death when your soul goes to heaven and the moment in the future when your body is raised from the dead. "The intermediate state" is what theologians call this time between death and the final resurrection.

HEAVEN WITHOUT YOUR BODY

Death, then, not only represents the end of physical life. It is also an unnatural and dreadful separation of soul and body, a ripping of our essential humanity, because we were originally created to be a unique being of both spirit and flesh: "The Lord God formed man from the dust of the ground and breathed into his nostrils the breath of life, and man became a living being" (Genesis 2:7).

In other words, *physical life* plus *spiritual life* equals *human life*. It was never God's original intent for the souls of human beings to remain in an intermediate, disembodied state. It follows, then, that spiritual life (a soul separated from its body) is not fully human life. The resurrection is, therefore, necessary to reinstate fully human life to everyone who has died.

Jesus Christ, as the firstfruits of the resurrection, represents the first full restoration of human life. When he died on the cross, he "gave up his spirit" (Matthew 27:50). In other words, something of his life left his body, and Jesus, too, entered the intermediate state, but not for long! The apostle Peter, in one of the more mysterious passages of the Bible, tells us that:

> Christ died for our sins once for all, the righteous for the unrighteous, to bring you to God. **He was put to death in the body but made alive by the Spirit,** through whom also he went and preached to the spirits in prison. 1 PETER 3:18-19

Whatever else this means, and Bible scholars are not certain, it suggests that Jesus was in a state of personal consciousness and purposeful life *separate* from his body, at least for a while. According to the ancient Christian creed familiar to people raised in traditional churches, Jesus was "born of the Virgin Mary, suffered under Pontius Pilate, was crucified dead and buried; *he descended into hell* [or Hades, the intermediate state]; the third day he rose again from the dead and ascended into heaven."

Jesus' descent into Hades is based on the passage above from 1 Peter—and on Ephesians 4:9: "What does 'he ascended' mean except that he also descended to the lower, earthly regions?" Obviously, all this is not so obvious, but it would appear that the spirit or life of Jesus left his body when he died. Yet the purpose of God for Jesus' afterlife was not complete until his physical body was raised from the dead three days later. Similarly, when Christian believers die, their conscious souls go immediately into the presence of God, but they will still be in an intermediate state, awaiting the final resurrection of their bodies and the full reconstruction of their humanity.

Unfortunately, lots of Christians never think about these things, nor are they aware that what they think about life after death may not be biblical. Like I said in the opening paragraphs of this chapter, the way many people think about heaven is somewhere between the Bible and "The Far Side."

I can't emphasize enough how important it is for us to think about life, death, and life after death in strictly biblical ways, leaving some of the unanswered questions to God. In my view, heaven and hell are not what I think they are or what I hope they will be. Life after death is what God says it is in his Word. Christian theologian Robert A. Morey summarizes this well:

Immortality and the Resurrection

When someone asks us if we believe in "the immortality of the soul," we respond by asking them to define their words because what they mean by "the immortality of the soul" will determine our answer.

Some are thinking of "essential immortality," which refers to a life having neither beginning nor end. According to the Bible, only God has essential immortality as an attribute of His being (1 Timothy 6:16). Since man begins at conception and does not come from eternity, he does not have essential immortality. Only God is from eternity to eternity (Psalms 90:1-2).

Other people have in their mind the Greek idea of the pre-existence of the soul or the Eastern ideas of transmigration or reincarnation. The Bible is clearly against such ideas. Man does not preexist his conception in the womb, and neither does he go through an endless cycle of rebirths....

Others may be thinking of "natural immortality," which views man as an autonomous and independent moral being through some kind of innate power. This also is erroneous, because man is always and absolutely dependent upon the Creator for this life as well as for the next life. Man should never be viewed as independent or autonomous. Life in this world and in the next must always be viewed as a gift from God.

Or again, some view death as "normal" and man's existence in an afterlife as "natural." While it is natural for angels to exist as spiritual entities, it is not natural for man to do so. Thus, man's death is not normal but a terrible ripping apart of what was never intended to be separated. The spiritual and physical sides of man are separated by death. And his existence as a spiritual entity alone is unnatural. *This is why the resurrection is necessary. Man was created as a physical-spiritual being and must ultimately be reconstituted in the same way. Death is an unnatural event and man's subsequent disembodied state [the intermediate state] is an unnatural existence which only the resurrection will remedy.*

ROBERT A. MOREY (Italics added.)[3]

THE RESURRECTION

It is God's intent, then, for us to live forever—"everlasting life," the Bible calls it—*but not without a physical body*, like Patrick Swayze's character in *Ghost*, or Ben Kenobi in *Star Wars*. Films like these may be fascinating, but they are *not* Christian. According to the Bible, everyone eventually will be raised from the dead, and the resurrection signals the end of the intermediate state. It's inevitable, because it is unnatural for our souls to remain disembodied.

Listen, I tell you a mystery: We will not all sleep, but we will all be changed—in a flash, in the twinkling of an eye, at the last trumpet. For the trumpet will sound, the dead will be raised imperishable, and we will be changed. For the perishable must clothe itself with the imperishable, and the mortal with immortality. When the perishable has been clothed with the imperishable, and the mortal with immortality, then the saying that is written will come true: "Death has been swallowed up in victory."

1 CORINTHIANS 15:51-54

THE FINAL STATE

The end of the intermediate state—the season of separation of the soul from the body—is the beginning of the final state: heaven and hell, both of which are described in some detail in the last couple of chapters of Revelation.

Then I saw a great white throne and him who was seated on it. Earth and sky fled from his presence, and there was no place for them. And I saw the dead, great and small, standing before the throne, and books were opened. Another book was opened, which is the book of life. The dead were judged according to what they had done as recorded in the books. The sea gave up the dead that were in it, and death and Hades gave up the dead that were in them, and each person was judged according to what he had done. Then death and Hades were thrown into the lake of fire. The lake of fire is the second death. If anyone's name was not found written in the book of life, he was thrown into the lake of fire. REVELATION 20:11-15

According to Revelation 20, immediately after the Great White Throne Judgment, the unrighteous—living and dead—are cast into hell. On the day of judgment, the temporary torment of Hades will become the eternal agony of the lake of fire, the final abode of Satan and his angels as well (see Revelation 20:7-10).

Hell is referred to in the Bible as "hell fire" (Matthew 5:22), a translation of the Greek word *gehenna*. When Jesus spoke of hell (gehenna), he was referring to the Valley of Hinnom, the garbage dump just outside the wall of ancient Jerusalem (see Mark 9:44).

Centuries before Christ, Gehenna was the site of pagan fire-worship during the time of the idolatrous Hebrew king, Ahaz. Later it became the dumping place of trash, animal carcasses, and even sewage. The fire there burned continually, and Jesus used this place—the worst imaginable place on earth—to describe the torment of separation from God.

Yes, there is an alternative to heaven. No matter what your conception of it may be, we know it will be separation from God and all that is holy and good. John Milton described it in *Paradise Lost:*

> A dungeon horrible on all sides round,
> As one great furnace, flamed;
> jet from those flames

No light, but rather darkness visible
Serv'd only to discover sights of woe,
Regions of sorrow, doleful shades, where peace
And rest can never dwell, hope never comes
That comes to all; but torture without end.

QUOTED BY BILLY GRAHAM[4]

HEAVEN

The afterlife is a real place, but most importantly, *heaven is where God is*—where he's with us and we're with him. The ordinary things we value so much in this life are lost in the extraordinary blessing of God's immediate and eternal presence.

I've often thought that going to heaven will be like being born. The safety and familiarity of my mother's womb was entirely forgotten in the dazzling sights and sounds of my new life. "Behold," God declares, "I will create new heavens and a new earth. The former things will not be remembered, nor will they come to mind" (Isaiah 65:17).

It's not that the memories of this life are unimportant. It's just that we have no point of reference in our fallen world for understanding what it's going to be like in heaven, in God's presence, in the presence of our loved ones, fulfilling the purposes of God forever. I can't even imagine what it's like to live forever, let alone understand what it means to live with God forever.

What, then, is heaven like? Heaven is personal, conscious, perpetual, and purposeful existence in the presence of God. We will recognize and enjoy family and friends as well. Will there be animals there? Or food? Or golf? The Bible is not clear on any of this! But we know from the Word of God that heaven is an indescribably wonderful place. Heaven is our real home.

Then I saw a new heaven and a new earth, for the first heaven and the first earth had passed away, and there was no longer any sea. I saw the Holy City, the new Jerusalem, coming down out of heaven from God... And I heard a loud voice from the throne saying, "Now the dwelling of God is with men, and he will live with them. They will be his people, and God himself will be with them and be their God. He will wipe every tear from their eyes. There will be no more death or mourning or crying or pain, for the old order of things has passed away."

He who was seated on the throne said, "I am making everything new!" REVELATION 21:1-5

AT HOME WITH OUR KING

Joni Eareckson Tada, paralyzed from the shoulders down from a diving accident in 1967, understands as well as any of us that heaven is our real home. For more on the subject of heaven, I recommend her latest book, *Heaven: Your Real Home*, in which she has a chapter titled, "At Home with Our King." Talking about life after death would be senseless without the perspective, that, ultimately, heaven is about eternity with Jesus.

Holy, Holy, Holy! All the saints adore Thee.
Casting down their golden crowns
around the glassy sea;
Cherubim and Seraphim
falling down before Thee,
Which wert and art and evermore shall be.

Above all, it will be Christ's coronation day.

I'm thrilled that we will enjoy the Marriage Supper of the Lamb with its feast of rich foods and the finest of wines, and we will delight in our reunion with loved ones, and, yes, it will be exhilarating to reign over angels and rule the earth with new bodies to boot. But I have to keep remembering it will not be *our* celebration. It will be *his.*

I could never dare keep those crowns for myself. Could you? We shall press in line with the great procession of the redeemed passing before the throne, an infinite cavalcade of nations and empires, age following age, Europe, Asia, Africa, North and South America, all standing shoulder to shoulder, the people of the islands of the seas in one happy parade, generations of the redeemed before the Cross and after, all bearing their diadems before God Almighty.

Then as Jesus rises from His throne before this great host, all crowns are lifted, all chimes ringing, and all hallelujahs hailing until the vocabulary of heavenly praise is exhausted. We will press our crowns against our breasts, look at one another, and say, "Now?"

"Now!" all will shout. Together we will raise our voices, not in four-part harmony, but perhaps in twelve-part, with the twenty-four elders as "they lay their crowns before the throne" (Revelation 4:10-11) and sing:

> *Crown Him with many crowns,*
> *the Lamb upon His throne:*
> *Hark! How the heavenly anthem drowns*
> *all music but its own!*
> *Awake, my soul, and sing*
> *of Him who died for thee,*
> *And hail Him as thy matchless king*
> *through all eternity.*

The universe will bow its knee and hail Jesus as King of Kings and Lord of Lords, when He raises His sword in victory over death, the devil, disease, and destruction.

In a breathless moment—an infinite moment—we will comprehend that the whole plan of redemption was merely the Father's way of securing for His Son...

A Bride.

A Family.

An Army.

An Inheritance.

But the crowning purpose of His plan will be to secure for the Son a grand chorus of Eternal Worshipers.

This is what I was made for. This is the answer to all the times I asked on earth, "Why has God chosen me? Why not someone else?" The response is simply, *I am the Father's gift to the Son....*

You and I were chosen to praise Him. It's that simple. What a shame that on earth we make it so complicated.

JONI EARECKSON TADA[5]

DO WE HAVE A CHOICE?

Are there options? Does it matter what we do in the here and now? If you're having doubts, don't bet your life on it!

If you've lost a loved one recently, the pain of that death is deep enough without having to think about heaven and hell, but that's the problem. When are we ever going to think about it? I am ashamed to say that I seek God most when I need him the most.

Billy Graham writes:

The Heidelberg Catechism, originally written in 1563 and used by Christians of many backgrounds, was a favorite of my father-in-law. On his study wall he had the first question and answer of the Heidelberg Catechism framed, which reads, "Q.1. What is your only comfort, in life and death? A. That I belong—body and soul, in life and death—not to myself but to my faithful Savior, Jesus Christ, who at the cost of his own blood has fully paid for all my sins and has completely freed me from the dominion of the devil; that he protects me so well that without the will of my Father in heaven not a hair can fall from my head; indeed, that everything must fit his purpose for my salvation. Therefore, by his Holy Spirit, he also assures me of eternal life, and makes me wholeheartedly willing and ready from now on to live for him."

...Many people are deceived by Satan into thinking that God is a vengeful task master, ready to send to hell all those who offend Him. They can see no hope. True, God does hate sin, but He loves the sinner. *Since we are all sinners, our only right for admission to heaven lies in the provision God made for our sins: His Son, Jesus Christ.* "For God so loved the world that he gave his one and only Son, that *whoever believes in him* shall not perish but have eternal life" (John 3:16).

BILLY GRAHAM (Italics added.)[6]

TWELVE

Faith and Hope
We Are Never Alone on Our Journey

Sorrow looks back,
worry looks around,
faith looks up.

AUTHOR UNKNOWN

What is faith? Do you have it? If you have it, do you have enough faith? Have you lost it?

A man jumped off a tall building. Some of the windows were open. As he sailed by on his way down, someone inside the building heard him say, "So far so good!"

Is that faith? Is that how you feel, like you're falling fast and there's no way to avoid a great crash?

Before you make a judgment about my stupid little story, think about this: the devil tried to get Jesus to jump off a tall building.

The devil led him to Jerusalem and had him stand on the highest point of the temple. "If you are the son of God," he said, "throw yourself down from here. For it is written:

"'He will command his angels concerning you to guard you carefully; they will lift you up in their hands, so that you will not strike your foot against a stone.'"

Jesus answered, "It says: 'Do not put the Lord your God to the test.'" LUKE 4:9-12

Do you feel as if your faith is tumbling? And do you have a terrible feeling that the angels are *not* going to catch you? Jesus said we are not to put God to the test. Are you feeling a role reversal, like God is putting *you* to the test? Do you resent that?

When all kinds of trials and temptations crowd into your lives, my brothers, don't resent them as intruders, but welcome them as friends! Realize that they come to test your faith and to produce in you the quality of endurance. But let the process go on until that endurance is fully developed, and you will find you have become [people] of mature character, [people] of integrity with no weak spots. And if, in the process, any of you does not know how to meet any particular problem he has only to ask God—who gives generously to all men without making them feel guilty—and he may be quite sure that the necessary wisdom will be given him. JAMES 1:2-5, PHILLIPS

I think my friend John Dalton understands something of what James is saying here. John wrote to me:

> To what extent is grief a positive experience? The litmus test would be to ask the question: Would I choose to live my life over again knowing that four of the six children conceived by us would experience untimely deaths? As a Christian, I would say, *Yes.*
>
> All the experiences of life give meaning to life, and each event is a unique opportunity to know God better. Grieving, like illness or imprisonment or any other human trauma, is essentially a spiritual experience.
>
> Compared with thirty years ago, is my life duller or brighter? Poorer or richer? Less or more meaningful? I have come to the conclusion that my life is certainly richer, although I have fewer simple answers to life's deeper questions.
>
> During the acute stage of my grieving, I thought I was going crazy. Nothing connected, and I was reduced to reaching out to a God I no longer understood. There were several biblical promises about God's rescue and protection that were especially meaningful to me. I was also touched by Jesus' commitment to me, to walk with me through the depths of pain yoked to my life. Christian friends spoke words of encouragement about how Jesus would sustain me, and though I received them suspiciously, God powerfully showed me that his promises were authentic, and that he was, indeed, working things out in my life.
>
> As I experienced the reality of God work, I found myself believing his promises more readily. I sensed a regeneration of my faith, my hope, and my love.

GOD'S ON YOUR SIDE!

God is on your side even when you are not sure what side you are on. Strange irony: If you're grieving the loss of a loved one, you probably have never thought about faith as much as you do now. And at the same time, you probably have never felt that you've had less faith. The story of St. Peter's infamous triple denial of Christ has been a huge encouragement to me. In one of the most shameful failures of Peter's life, Jesus had already prayed in advance that his faith wouldn't fail. And that's why it didn't.

Simon, Simon, Satan has asked to sift you as wheat. **But I have prayed for you, Simon, that your faith may not fail**. LUKE 22:31-32

It's hard for some people to believe that God keeps caring for them even when their faith is fizzling. If you are bereaved, you're probably having a hard time believing anything right now, so you need all the encouragement you can get.

If we are faithless, he will remain faithful, for he cannot disown himself. 2 TIMOTHY 2:13

You see, faith is certainly about your response to God, but it's much bigger than that. It's about God working in you, especially when you need him the most. Paul said confidently:

If God is for us, who can be against us? He who did not spare his own Son, but gave him up for us all—how will he not also, along with him, graciously give us all things?... Who is he that condemns? Christ Jesus, who died—more than that, who was raised to life—**is at the right hand of God and is also interceding for us**. Who shall separate us from the love of Christ? Shall trouble or hardship or persecution or famine or nakedness or danger or sword? ...No, **in all these things we are more than conquerors through him who loved us**. For I am convinced that **neither death nor life**, neither angels nor demons, neither the present nor the future, nor any powers, neither height nor depth, nor anything else in all creation, will be able to separate us from the love of God that is in Christ Jesus our Lord. ROMANS 8:31-39

So what do you say to that? Is God on your side? Yes! In a chapter on faith you need to know this up front, because like everyone else, you are probably thinking much more about *your need for faith in God* than about *God's faithfulness to you.* Here are more Bible verses to feed your starving soul:

> In the same way, the Spirit helps us in our weakness. We do not know what we ought to pray, but the Spirit himself intercedes for us with groans that words cannot express. ROMANS 8:26

> I always pray with joy...being confident of this, that he who began a good work in you will carry it on to completion until the day of Christ Jesus. PHILIPPIANS 1:4-6

Kept by the Power of God

The words from which I speak, you will find in 1 Peter 1:5. The third, fourth, and fifth verses are: "Blessed be the God and Father of our Lord Jesus Christ which...hath begotten us again unto a lively hope by the resurrection of Jesus Christ from the dead, to an inheritance incorruptible...reserved in heaven for you, who are kept by the power of God through faith unto salvation."

There we have two wonderful, blessed truths about the keeping by which a believer is kept unto salvation. One truth is, *Kept by the power of God*; and the other truth is, *Kept through faith.* We should look at the two sides—at God's side and His almighty power, offered to us to be our Keeper every moment of the day; and at the human side, we have nothing to do but in faith to let God do His keeping work....

Now, as to the first part of this keeping, there is no doubt and no question. God keeps the inheritance in Heaven very wonderfully and perfectly, and it is waiting there safely. And the same God keeps me for the inheritance...

You know it is very foolish of a father to take great trouble to have an inheritance for his children, and to keep it for them, if he does not keep them for it. What would you think of a man spending his whole time and making every sacrifice to amass money, and as he gets his tens of thousands, you ask him why it is that he sacrifices himself so, and his answer is: "I want to leave my children a large inheritance, and I am keeping it for them"—if you were then to hear that that man takes no trouble to educate his children, that he allows them to run upon the street wild, and to go on in paths of sin and ignorance and folly, what would you think of him?... [Yet] there are so many Christians who think: "My God is keeping the inheritance for me"; but they cannot believe: "My God is keeping me for that inheritance." The same power, the same love, the same God [does both!]....

What is kept? *You* are kept. How much of you? The whole being. Does God keep one part of you and not another? No. Some people have an idea that this is a sort of vague, general keeping, and that God will keep them in such a way that when they die they will get to Heaven. But they do not apply that word *kept* to everything in their being and nature. And yet that is what God wants.

ANDREW MURRAY[1]

I'm never sure of the future, but I am profoundly reassured of God's care for me when I think about the wonderful tapestry of my life. I may have my doubts about how it's all going to turn out, but when I look back, it is so evident that nothing in my life has been accidental. God has taken the worst times of my life and purposefully used them to change me. Somehow, all things really do work together for good for those who love God.

No discipline seems pleasant at the time, but painful. Later on, however, it produces a harvest of righteousness and peace for those who have been trained by it. HEBREWS 12:11

In retrospect, I can now see how God was working most significantly in my life, and his presence was never nearer, than during those times when I *least* felt his providence. Amazing! I thank God that my faith doesn't depend solely on my own personal spiritual energy. Jesus is praying for me that my faith won't fail, just like he did for Peter. And he's praying for your faith, too. Right now.

John Dalton feels the same way:

Looking back is so much fun. [Could a man who lost four children, one to abortion, actually say this? Why would he? He also says...] I realize that I really don't know very much about the subject of grief. In hindsight, though, I can see more clearly, and I have fewer questions about what's behind me than I do about what's in front of me.

It is one thing to claim God's promises, but the real issue is to walk out his promises with him. Healing waters that are a mile wide and an inch deep will dry up quickly, but the deepening of the waters will last a lifetime. Even now, after all the years of deepening, I am not entirely sure how the deepening process is accomplished. I do know, however, that I can't make it happen in my head, and I do know that a huge part of it is in the hands of God, in his will and timing. And sometimes he takes a terribly long time.

I used to play a musical instrument. After months of practicing without any sense of progress, I would suddenly find myself doing things musically I could not do just a few days before.

Grieving Christians, too, will endure long periods of spiritual impasse, broken by abrupt bursts of energy, life, and a deeper communion with the heavenly Father. Again, I'm not sure anyone understands precisely how this works, except by faithfully waiting and watching for it to happen. When I think I'm making little or no progress in the healing process, I suddenly find myself relating to my loss in new and positive ways. And I know God has done something special.

Therefore you must wear the whole armor of God that you may be able to resist evil in its day of power, and that even when you have fought to a **standstill** you may **still stand** your ground.
EPHESIANS 6:13, PHILLIPS

FOUR KINDS OF FAITH

If it had not occurred to you until now (until this time of terrible testing in your life), faith and how it works is not so easily understood. "You just have to believe," someone tells you. But how? How much? How long? In what way? Before your loss, you didn't ask yourself those questions. Faith seemed simple enough. But now, in your pain and anger, everything seems so complicated and confusing.

You need to know that even writers of the Scriptures wrestled with what it meant to trust God in a world where there are more questions than answers. As I have read and studied the Bible, I have come to the conclusion that there are different "kinds" of faith.

Faith to get saved. The *first* "kind" of faith is basic to Christianity: *faith to save*. This is what you do to accept Christ, but somehow, unexplainably, it goes beyond what *you* do. Every one of us who knows Jesus could tell a story about how we decided to become a Christian. But we would also have to admit we didn't just find God, He found us. His providence brought us to the point of decision.

"No one can come to me," Jesus declared, "unless the Father who sent me draws him" (John 6:44). Does the word *draw* sound gentle? Actually, in the original language of the New Testament, the word means "drag"! No one comes to the Son unless the Father drags him!

Now I don't think this means that God forces anyone to become a Christian, but you know from your own life that you were not deeply willing to make Jesus your Savior and Lord. Becoming a Christian is not something that comes naturally. God had to allow some things to happen around you to get your attention, to bring you to the point where you were willing to open your life to his grace.

The comfort in this for the grieving Christian is that God is still in control, even when you feel out of control. What happens to you, starting with the moment you are saved, has everything to do with God's grace, and if God was willing to extend his grace to you while you are still his enemy, how much more now that you are his friend. If grace works to save us forever, it will work to save you today.

For it is by grace you have been saved, through faith—and this not from yourselves, it is the gift of God—not by works, so that no one can boast. For we are God's workmanship, created in Christ Jesus to do good works, which God prepared in advance for us to do. EPHESIANS 2:8-10

Faith to receive. The first kind of faith, then, is faith—with God's intervention and help—to believe in Jesus for the forgiveness of your sins. It is faith to be born again. The *second* kind is *faith to receive.* After you become a Christian, you learn that believing God is something you need to do daily, and you discover that faith gets results as you take the promises of God's Word into your life.

It's impossible to please God apart from faith. Why? Because anyone who wants to approach God must believe both that he exists **and** that he cares enough to respond to those who seek him.

HEBREWS 11:6, *THE MESSAGE*

Doubt of God's goodness creates the terror of aloneness in an unreliable world, which leads to rage against God for doing so little to protect us from suffering.

LARRY CRABB[2]

Trust—Here and Now

Though you have been made right with God, you may not yet have entered into the rest of God. Your heart may be in a vast wilderness—wandering because of unbelief.

Many people who receive eternal life through faith in Christ never learn to trust Christ for the temporal things of life. We say, "O, I believe God. I believe that when I step out of this world he is going to take me into everlasting mansions." But if we can't believe that God can take care of us for the next six months, how can we believe that God can take care of us forever?

From analyzing his mountains of mail, a nationally known minister with a syndicated column in hundreds of newspapers across the country says that people are concerned with two main problems: fear and worry.

But it doesn't have to be that way. The book *Hudson Taylor's Spiritual Secret* tells the story of a life lived with all the trappings taken away. Hudson Taylor, the great missionary to China and founder of the China Inland Mission, learned a great and simple spiritual secret: Just as he had trusted Christ and his promises for eternal life through faith, he could also by faith claim the promises of God and find the rest of God right here in this life.

D. JAMES KENNEDY[3]

The gift of faith. The third kind of faith is *the gift of faith*. In 1 Corinthians 12:8-10, Paul lists nine manifestations of the Holy Spirit, one of which is "faith." The *Weymouth Translation* renders this word "special faith."[4] I call it "mountain-moving faith," the kind Paul mentions a little later in 1 Corinthians 13:2: "...and if I have faith that can move mountains [the greatest, most spectacular kind], but have not love, I am nothing."

Some people just seem to be gifted with outbursts of faith followed by significant miracles, the kind you hear about on Christian television and which make you wonder contritely, "Maybe if I had that kind of faith, my loved one would not have died."

But take heart! Maybe it wasn't the failure of your faith after all. Maybe the testimony you heard in church, or on a Christian TV program, was God working in a special way through the *gift* of faith, which according to 1 Corinthians 12 is *not* for every Christian in every situation.

> Now to each one the manifestation of the Spirit is given for the common good. **To one** there is given through the Spirit the message of wisdom, **to another** the message of knowledge by means of the same Spirit, **to another faith** by the same Spirit, **to another** gifts of healing by that one Spirit, **to another** miraculous powers, **to another** prophecy, **to another** the ability to distinguish between spirits, **to another** the ability to speak in different kinds of tongues, and **to still another** the interpretation of tongues. All these are the work of one and the same Spirit, and **he gives them to each one, just as he determines.** 1 CORINTHIANS 12:7-11

It is quite logical to conclude, from this Scripture, that no one has all the gifts, which means that only some have the gift of faith. On the other hand, in Galatians 5:22-23, faith is one of the nine *fruit* of the Spirit:

> But the fruit of the Spirit is love, joy, peace, patience, kindness, goodness, **faithfulness** [same Greek word that's used in 1 Corinthians 12], gentleness and self-control... Those who belong to Christ Jesus have crucified the sinful nature with its passions and desires. Since we live by the Spirit, let us keep in step with the Spirit. GALATIANS 5:22-25

The way I read this, every Christian should have all nine fruit. So the emphasis in 1 Corinthians 12 is different from Paul's emphasis in Galatians 5. Nine gifts in 1 Corinthians 12. Nine fruit in Galatians 5. Interestingly, faith is the only term that appears in both lists, and faith *as a gift* of the Spirit *is not* for everyone, while faith *as a fruit* of the Spirit *is* for everyone. There really are different kinds of faith, in that faith expresses itself differently through different people.

Why is this so important to talk about? Because when you run into someone with the *gift* of faith, there's always the danger that you're going to feel like your faith is marginal. The gift of faith in someone else can be so powerful, so unusual, so full of God, that it makes you feel like a spiritual wimp. And guilty too. To put it another way, it may *look like* some people have more faith than others when they really don't. They just have the gift of faith.

Faithfulness. The fourth kind of faith is *faithfulness*. I'm convinced that this is the kind of faith in Galatians 5:22, as suggested by the NIV translation: "the fruit of the Spirit is... *faithfulness*." Faithfulness means trusting God even when you have every reason not to, like Job who said (I'm paraphrasing), "Even if God kills me, I'm still going to praise him."

> At this [when he heard of the death of his children], Job got up and tore his robe and shaved his head. Then he fell to the ground in worship and said:
> "Naked I came from my mother's womb,
>   and naked will I depart.
> The Lord gave and the Lord has taken away;
>   may the name of the Lord be praised."
> In all this, Job did not sin by charging God with wrongdoing.
> JOB 1:20-22

From the way some Christians talk about it, you'd think faith is a quick fix. Of course, that's certainly not a biblical concept, but we are an impatient people, and sometimes we look at faith as a kind of push-button or instant-credit Christianity. We need to be reminded, then, that there's nothing magical about faith, and when we believe God for something, results are rarely instantaneous. *Especially when you are grieving.*

Faithfulness is faith for the long term. Faithfulness is trusting God when your faith isn't getting what you want when you want it.

> Though the fig tree does not bud
> and there are no grapes on the vines,
> though the olive crop fails
> and the fields produce no food,
> though there are no sheep in the pen
> and no cattle in the stalls,
> yet I will rejoice in the Lord,
> I will be joyful in God my Savior.
>
> The Sovereign Lord is my strength;
> he makes my feet like the feet of a deer,
> he enables me to go on the heights. HABAKKUK 3:17-19

Shadrach, Meshach and Abednego replied to the king, "O Nebuchadnezzar, we do not need to defend ourselves before you in this matter. If we are thrown into the blazing furnace, the God we serve is able to save us from it, and he will rescue us from your hand, O king [Faith!]. But even if he does not, we want you to know, O king, that we will not serve your gods or worship the image of gold you have set up [Faithfulness!]." DANIEL 3:16-18

Sometimes it seems like faith is believing God for what you want, hoping it's what God wants too. Faithfulness is letting God be God. A favorite professor of mine at Fuller seminary, Ray Anderson, tells the story of his parents' unquestioning faith in God—and their acceptance of death, even tragic death.

Unquestioning Faith

On a lazy, summer Sunday afternoon, without apparent pre-meditation, my parents would suddenly announce a trip to the local rural cemetery for the purpose of tending some family grave sites. Of course we children were included. It was not a long trip, for the cemetery adjoined the farm on which we lived on the flat prairie-land of middle America.

The simple rituals of pulling some weeds, clipping some grass and digging up the soil around a straggling, flowering plant were quickly accomplished, and served only as a pretext for the visit, as it usually turned out.

Trailing behind, as my parents wandered from grave site to grave site, I heard the litany of their commentary on the dead. "Here's where the Torstensons are buried. Wasn't she a Carlson girl who came over with her parents from the old country, and didn't they homestead the quarter section next to the old Anderson farm where I was born?" my father would ask.

And so it went. These were not questions, but statements. Statements about a community in which the boundary between the living and the dead lost its sharp edge of terror. This was a mystery which was part of the fabric of life. What this small boy experienced was the easy familiarity with which this uncanny boundary was traversed. But even more, what was experienced was the wordless testimony that this excursion was an event in which their faith was enacted. Implicit in this patriarchal pageantry was a statement about what they believed; and death was not alien to this belief system.

What did my father think about when he tended the grave sites and contemplated the plot where he himself would one day be buried? Did he have anxiety? Did he fear that death would annihilate all of the meaning of his life to that point?...

What did he think when he passed the small grave marker and commented, "Yes, and here is the two-year-old Peterson boy; he was kicked in the head by a cow and died that very night"? Had he ever questioned the fairness of that? Had he ever questioned God about that?

I don't know. He never said. Death and God were the two things that were never openly questioned. Perhaps the question and the answer had become so fused that faith was as simple as a Sunday afternoon walk in the cemetery and planting a straight row of corn.

RAY ANDERSON[5]

FAITH TO MAKE IT THROUGH

Faithfulness is faith that makes it through, faith that *endures*. The New Testament Greek term most often translated "endure" is a combination of two other words which mean "to remain under." To endure is to be under something, like the weight of some difficult circumstance, but to keep pressing forward anyway. In the ancient Greek world, endurance was considered a primary virtue and had the sense of courageous persistence.

"Patience is a virtue." We've all heard that one from our mothers and grandmothers, but sometimes people think of patience as nothing more than passive resignation to the frustration of the moment. It's giving up and giving in—and being nice about it. "Well," we sigh, "that's just the way it is, and I can't do anything about it"—as in long lines at the grocery store or rush hour traffic on the freeway.

Not that patience isn't a virtue, but endurance is more long term, as in long-suffering, a word that's often used in the old King James Bible to translate the Greek word *hupomone*. Endurance is active and energetic resistance, with an eye on the finish line, like an Olympic runner.

Have you ever watched a marathon? Or, even worse, an Ironman competition? Each year in Hawaii, hundreds of endurance fanatics gather for what has to be the most grueling test of stamina and will

193

in the known universe. The competitors run a full marathon, twenty-six miles—*after* swimming miles across Kailua Bay *and* cycling a couple hours up and down the Big Island's hot Kona Coast. You need more than patience to be an Ironman. You need endurance. Mega-endurance! You need a willful and deliberate commitment to endure the pain and press through to the end.

St. Paul even wrote about the need to endure:

Do you not know that in a race all the runners run, but only one gets the prize? Run in such a way as to get the prize. Everyone who competes in the games goes into strict training. They do it to get a crown that will not last; but we do it to get a crown that will last forever. Therefore I do not run like a man running aimlessly; I do not fight like a man beating the air.

1 CORINTHIANS 9:24-26

Faithfulness is faith that endures, in spite of what you are "remaining under," in spite of everything in your mind and emotions screaming, "Give up! Give in! You gotta quit!"

The Faith to Persevere

"Because you have kept My command to persevere..." (Revelation 3:10 NKJV).

Perseverance means more than endurance—more than simply holding on to the end. A saint's life is in the hands of God like a bow and arrow in the hands of an archer. God is aiming at something the saint cannot see, but our Lord continues to stretch and strain, and every once in a while the saint says, "I can't take any more." Yet God pays no attention; He goes on stretching until His purpose is in sight, and then He lets the arrow fly. Entrust yourself to God's hands. Is there something in your life for which you need perseverance right now? Maintain your intimate relationship with Jesus Christ through the perseverance of faith. Proclaim as Job did, "Though He slay me, yet will I trust Him" (Job 13:15).

Faith is not some weak and pitiful emotion, but is strong and vigorous confidence built on the fact that God is holy love. And even though you cannot see Him right now and cannot understand what He is doing, you know *Him*. Disaster occurs in your life when you lack the mental composure that comes from establishing yourself on the eternal truth that God is holy love. Faith is the supreme effort of your life—throwing yourself with abandon and total confidence upon God.

God ventured His all in Jesus Christ to save us, and now He wants us to venture our all with total abandoned confidence in Him. There are areas in our lives where that faith has not worked in us as yet—places still untouched by the life of God. There were none of those places in Jesus Christ's life, and there are to be none in ours. Jesus prayed, "This is eternal life, that they may know You..." (John 17:3). The real meaning of eternal life is a life that can face anything it has to face without wavering. If we will take this view, life will become one great romance—a glorious opportunity of seeing wonderful things all the time. God is disciplining us into this central place of power.

OSWALD CHAMBERS[6]

ENDURING TO THE END

He who stands firm to the end will be saved. MATTHEW 10:22

"How can I endure to the end?"

I know that's what you're thinking, and I have a simple answer: *One day at a time.*

I have two brothers who live on the other side of the Phoenix metro area. It's about a fifty-minute drive in good traffic. Often, when I make that drive, I think back to the long commute I made every day for two years when we first started Word of Grace, where I serve as senior pastor.

I've said to myself, "How did I ever do that?" It's simple: one mile at a time, one day at a time.

How do people survive the Ironman triathlon in Hawaii? One stroke, one stride at a time.

How do you make it through your grief? One day at a time. Sometimes one hour at a time.

Did you make it this far?

Did you make it through yesterday?

Did you make it through last week?

Then, God helping you, you're going to make it through today. And this week. And this month.

God will give you grace one day at a time. Jesus said,

Therefore, do not worry about tomorrow, for tomorrow will worry about itself. Each day has enough trouble of its own.

MATTHEW 6:34

Sing to the Lord, you saints of his;
    praise his holy name.
For his anger lasts only a moment,
    but his favor lasts a lifetime;
    weeping may remain for a night,
    but rejoicing comes in the morning. PSALMS 30:4-5

HOPE: THE ANSWER TO THE PROBLEM OF FAITH

Hope is passion for what is possible.

KIERKEGAARD

We were of the opinion that hope was for the non-Christian but the Christian had something better which was faith.

TREVOR CHANDLER[7]

Have you ever heard someone say, "I have hope, but I don't have faith"? Or, "I only have a *vague* hope." They say it like hope is something less than faith, and you almost want to rebuke them for their unbelief.

But I've done some careful thinking about hope, and I've discovered some liberating things. Although both hope and faith are necessary elements of the Christian life, in some ways hope is even more basic than faith. Hope, as it is used in the Bible, is not just wishful thinking.

Faith has to do with the present: "Now faith is being sure of what we hope for and certain of what we do not see" (Hebrews 11:1). Hope, on the other hand, has to do with the future. Faith has to do with what *is*. Hope has to do with what *will be*.

If faith, then, is grounded in what we hope for, it's perfectly correct to say, "I have hope, but I don't have faith." I have come to the conclusion that you can have hope without faith, but you can never have faith without hope.

We always thank God, the Father of our Lord Jesus Christ, when we pray for you, because we have heard of your **faith** in Christ Jesus and of the love you have for all the saints—[and listen to this!] **the faith and love that spring from the hope** that is stored up for you in heaven. COLOSSIANS 1:3-5

Hope is the anchor of faith. Faith is tied to hope, and hope is tied to the future. Faith brings the hope of the future into the present. *Faith is the way you live in the unpleasant present because of what you know is in the glorious future!*

And what's in the future? *God!* The future belongs to God. We can be faithful until we die, because hope takes us beyond death! In fact, the Bible even calls the resurrection from the dead our "blessed hope."[8]

This is a trustworthy saying that deserves full acceptance (and for this we labor and strive), that we have put our **hope** in the living God, who is the Savior of all men, especially of those who believe. 1 TIMOTHY 4:9-10

To them God has chosen to make known among the Gentiles the glorious riches of this mystery, **which is Christ in you, the hope of glory.** COLOSSIANS 1:27

We continually remember before our God and Father your work **produced by faith**, your labor **prompted by love**, and your endurance **inspired by hope** in our Lord Jesus Christ.

1 THESSALONIANS 1:3

Hope, then, is not the shallow end of faith. It is the anchor and energy of faithfulness and endurance in the face of life's greatest demands. "Why art thou cast down, oh my soul?... *Hope now in God!*" (Psalms 42:5 KJV)

THIRTEEN

Unsolved Mysteries
Why, God?

Verily Thou art a God that hidest Thyself, O
God of Israel, the Savior.

ISAIAH 45:15, KJV

We are not given explanations but, to hearts
open to receive it, a more precious revelation of
the heart of our loving Lord.

ELISABETH ELLIOT

If faith works, why doesn't it?

I was speaking on the power of the Holy Spirit—how you can believe God for miracles. After the meeting, a woman confined to a wheelchair confronted me, "I have a lot of trouble with the power of the Holy Spirit."

I knew I was in deep water.

"Let me guess that you have had lots of people pray for your healing," I responded, as sensitively as I could.

"Yes," she said, and nodded. "It seems like hundreds." And obviously she had not been healed.

"How long have you been in a wheelchair?" I asked.

"Twenty years," she replied with a sigh. "I was working in a convenience market. Some guy came in to rob the store and shot me. The bullet passed through my spinal cord."

I could tell she was weary of telling the story.

Sensing her profound pain, I ventured a dangerous question: "Have there been times you wished the bullet had taken your life?"

Her lips tightened as she nodded yes again.

Why, God? If faith works, why is this woman still waiting to be healed?

Why, God? If we believe and trust in you, why do our loved ones die? Why do they die tragically? Violently?

In the previous chapter, I discussed four kinds (or expressions) of faith: saving faith, faith to receive, the gift of faith, and faith to endure. If you haven't already done so, I suggest you read that chapter *before* you read this one.

In this chapter[1] I want to talk a little more about the faith issue and, at the risk of moralizing (see chapter six), try to answer the unanswerable questions, the great unsolved mysteries.

Why did this happen?

Where is God in it all?

Would things have been different if I had had more faith?

Or been more righteous?

Or prayed more?

The ABC's of Suffering

A member of my church handed me this little story,

An elderly gentleman passed his granddaughter's room one night and overheard her repeating the alphabet in an oddly reverent way. "What on earth are you up to?" he asked.

"I'm saying my prayers," explained the little girl. "But I can't think of exactly the right words tonight, so I'm just saying all the letters. God will put them together for me, because he knows what I'm thinking."[2]

I wonder if Jesus had something like this in mind when he announced, "I am the Alpha and the Omega [the first and last letters of the Greek alphabet], the Beginning and the End" (Revelation 21:6). Jesus is everything in the middle, too. He is God's encyclopedia of answers for human problems.

We can't always explain what happens to us and others, but God can. And someday he will.

In the meantime, we have to accept the fact that life can be a real mess and impossible to explain.

WHY?

It is the glory of God to conceal a matter. PROVERBS 25:2

The secret things belong to the Lord our God.

DEUTERONOMY 29:29

As you do not know the path of the wind, or how the body is formed in a mother's womb, so you cannot understand the work of God, the Maker of all things. ECCLESIASTES 11:5

"For my thoughts are not your thoughts, neither are your ways my ways," declares the Lord. "As the heavens are higher than the earth, so are my ways higher than your ways and my thoughts than your thoughts." ISAIAH 55:8-9

Sometimes things seem so random and senseless, all we can do is groan. The apostle Paul actually discusses this in Romans 8, which is considered by many to be one of the most important chapters in the Bible.

> The creation waits in eager expectation for the sons of God to be revealed. For the creation was subjected to frustration, not by its own choice, but by the will of the one who subjected it, in hope that the creation itself will be liberated from its bondage to decay and brought into the glorious freedom of the children of God.
> We know that the whole creation has been groaning as in the pains of childbirth right up to the present time. Not only so, but we ourselves, who have the firstfruits of the Spirit, groan inwardly as we wait eagerly for our adoption as sons, the redemption of our bodies. ROMANS 8:19-23

Simply stated—and this is the reality we often ignore—the creation was subjected to frustration. Life is not what it ought to be nor what it will be. Life is difficult at best, and we are all groaning for a better world. The whole world groans. Not only is there pain, but at times there is no way to explain the pain, except to say that's just the way it is.

SPEECHLESS GROANING

I was asked to do a funeral for a family I did not know. It was as sad a service as I have ever seen. A mother and her twenty-four-year-old invalid child were in a serious car accident. The mother was killed. At the close of the service, a family member rolled the daughter's wheelchair to the side of the coffin.

I wasn't sure the child could understand what was happening, until she broke into the most pathetic weeping I have ever heard. I cried. Everyone cried. The woman in the coffin had spent all her waking hours lovingly caring for a human being who would now probably have to be institutionalized.

Can anyone even begin to explain such an agonizing loss?

Can you hear the speechless groans?

Why, God?

It's no wonder that Paul declared, "I consider that our present sufferings are not worth comparing with the glory that will be revealed in us." Paul is idealistic in the proper sense, but he is also realistic. He holds out no hope that this life will be the ultimate source of happiness. Life is so difficult at times that we don't know what to say. We don't even know what to pray.

> In the same way, the Spirit helps us in our weakness. We do not know what we ought to pray, but the Spirit himself intercedes for us with groans that words cannot express. ROMANS 8:26

According to Romans 8, the only hope to be heard in the echoes of our hollow groans is God's threefold provision: *First*, the certainty of the resurrection and ultimate renewal of the entire universe (see above in Romans 8:20-23); *second*, the promise that somehow everything will work together for good for those who love God (see Romans 8:28); and *third*, the ceaseless, unconditional prayers of the Holy Spirit over us.

> And he who searches our hearts knows the mind of the Spirit, because the Spirit intercedes for the saints in accordance with God's will. ROMANS 8:27

The nature of this crazy world is such that many tragedies defy explanation. All we can do is groan. When we don't know what to say, or what to pray, or how to pray, the Spirit of God brings our needs before the heavenly Father with a groaning of empathy, hope, and release that overpowers the groanings of this dark, confusing world.

THE GUILT OF IT ALL

A woman in our church called for comfort and to ask if I would conduct her husband's funeral. Years before, this Christian man had been seriously injured in a car wreck. He had been driving while intoxicated. After the accident, his life became a roller coaster of seizures and more drinking. It was a seizure that finally killed him.

His wife had prayed for years. He prayed, too—when he was not overwhelmed with guilt.

So why did he die?

Prayer is supposed to change things.

Did their faith fail?

Did Jesus fail her?

Did the devil win?

When faith doesn't "work," it raises perhaps the most difficult issues of the Christian life. At the root is the age-old question, "Why do bad things happen to good people?"

If we are "good," why doesn't God protect us?

Why do our prayers of faith go unanswered?

Why does evil seem to win?

As you have probably already concluded, I don't have all the answers! But I've thought about this a lot, and I have some ideas that have helped me personally.

Let me begin by affirming a basic principle of the Bible: *Faith works.* Faith produces results. If we believe, the Bible assures us, things will happen in our favor.

Without faith it is impossible to please God, because anyone who comes to him must believe that he exists and that he rewards those who earnestly seek him. HEBREWS 11:6

I diagram it this way:

Faith ————> Results

Faith produces results. In Hebrews 11, the sacred writer underscores this simple logic with numerous stories of faith from the Old Testament:

… *by faith* Abel, Enoch, Abraham, Isaac, Joseph, Moses…

… *by faith*, the people passed through the Red sea.

… *by faith* the walls of Jericho fell.

… *by faith* Rahab was *not* killed.

… *through faith* Gideon, Barak, Samson, Jephthah, David, Samuel, and the prophets conquered kingdoms, administered justice, and *gained what was promised* (see verse 33).

The point of Hebrews 11, of course, is to build my faith. The fact is, faith works. What we do or don't do, what we believe or don't believe—and how much we believe—has a lot to do with what happens to us. Lots of scriptures make this clear:

> Do not be deceived: God cannot be mocked. A man reaps what he sows. GALATIANS 6:7

> So we see that [the Israelites] were not able to enter [the Promised Land] because of their unbelief. HEBREWS 3:19

> [Jesus] could not do any miracles there, except lay his hands on a few sick people and heal them. And he was amazed at their lack of faith. MARK 6:5-6

> "Have faith in God," Jesus answered. "I tell you the truth, if anyone says to this mountain, 'Go, throw yourself into the sea,' and does not doubt in his heart but believes that what he says will happen, it will be done for him. Therefore I tell you, whatever you ask for in prayer, believe that you have received it, and it will be yours." MARK 11:22-24

Faith is supposed to work, but when it isn't working, or when it doesn't *seem* to be working, reading Hebrews 11 and these other Bible verses could have an adverse affect. You could get very discouraged. You could come to the conclusion that something's wrong with you, and here's how: If the Bible tells you that faith produces results, then simple logic also tells you that when things go wrong there must necessarily be something wrong with your faith.

When tragedy strikes we reverse the formula and come to one or more of four crippling conclusions:

1. No results ———→ No faith

No results, we presume, means not enough faith. So we blame ourselves. We feel guilt, condemnation. Or:

2. No results ──────► The devil wins

No results, we deduce, means that evil has triumphed, so we blame the devil, which is really nothing more than an indirect way to blame ourselves. We should have resisted him, right?

Or it's an indirect way to blame God because he should have protected us:

3. No results ──────► God is powerless
Or:

4. No results ──────► God is not loving

No results, we think to ourselves, means that God does not really care, because if he did, he wouldn't have allowed this to happen. The effect of all this is discouragement or alarm or a sense of failure and defeat or even a waning trust in God.

John Dalton, who has shared honestly throughout this book about his unspeakable loss of his children, is open about his personal confusion about these issues:

> In my own grieving experience, there are two areas which remain a great mystery to me, and continue to be the source of unanswered questions. The first is whether the loss of my three children was the direct result of my disobedience and God's discipline, or was it perhaps God's refining process working on my immaturity?
>
> I know that God disciplines those he loves, but the good and evil events of life seem to fall randomly on both the righteous and the wicked. I am reluctant to accept the fact that God would actually use the death of my children to discipline me, and yet I have to admit that I have definitely walked closer to the Lord over the past twenty years. I might cautiously believe that God was disciplining me, but I could not bring myself to suggest that to someone else.
>
> I may not be right in this, but I am convinced that growth in Christ is an outgrowth of all of life's experiences. I guess there is just a tension here I have to live with, because while I do not

blame God for what has happened in my family, I must confess my own waywardness, selfishness, and lack of love.

The second question is whether Satan caused this. This was first suggested by a pastor friend of mine at the time of Tom's mountaineering accident. This raised very difficult issues for me: Had I not prayed earnestly enough for protection for my family? Where were the angels? While I confess my lack of prayer and my inability to discern the deeper issues of the Spirit in my son's death, I cannot and do not take on guilt over this issue.

Was Tom's death the result of a battle with evil? I just don't know, although I do not presume it to be so. I can, however, speak with confidence about the reality of spiritual warfare *after* the deaths of our children. During our times of intense pain and suffering, and during the bewilderment that accompanied our grieving, we seemed so vulnerable to the intrusion of evil.

I know that God is sovereign. He will do whatever he chooses to do, to prevent or to allow. This means I must accept his dominion over my life and family, and not get entangled in fruitless discussions about cause and effect. I have to recognize—with awe and wonder—that God is God.

So while the exact cause of my loss is not clear to me, God's healing is, because I know him.

HELP!

Actually, help is right there in Hebrews 11. Let's get back to that text. Hebrews 11 is not only about how faith works, it's about how faith is still faith even when it doesn't produce the results we expect. Notice the change of pace in the middle of verse 35, where the list of "successful" saints ends with the first half of the verse (you may want to open your Bible to see this in context):

> Women received back their dead, raised to life again. **Others** were tortured and refused to be released.... They were stoned; they were sawed in two; they were put to death by the sword. They went about in sheepskins and goatskins, destitute, persecuted and mistreated. HEBREWS 11:35-37

Destitute?! Did their faith fail? Did the devil win? No! In fact, the Bible tells us that these "were all commended for their faith, yet none of them received what had been promised" (verse 39). Faith, then, is not measured by tangible results alone. Sometimes God commends us for our faithfulness and perseverance, even when there are no visible results!

I'll say it again: *Faith produces results, but genuine faith is not measured by results alone.* God is especially pleased with *faithfulness,* even when we don't see any results. This verse was scratched into a basement wall by one of the victims of the Holocaust:

I believe in the sun—even when it does not shine.
I believe in love—even when it is not shown.
I believe in God—even when he is silent.

A survivor of the Holocaust wrote:

Though He Slay Me...

I have followed Him even when He rejected me. I have followed His commandments even when He has castigated me for it; I have loved Him and I love Him even when He hurls me to the earth, tortures me to death, makes me the object of shame and ridicule.... God of Israel...You have done everything to make me stop believing in You. Now lest it seem to You that You will succeed by these tribulations to drive me from the right path, I notify You, my God and God of my fathers that it will not avail You in the least! You may insult me. You may castigate me. You may take from me all that I cherish and hold dear in this world. You may torture me to death—I shall believe in You, I shall love You no matter what You do to test me!

And these are my last words to You, my wrathful God: nothing will avail You in the least. You have done everything to make me renounce You, to make me lose faith in You, but I die exactly as I have lived, a believer!

THEODOR HERZL[3]

That sounds like the three men in the fiery furnace:

Shadrach, Meshach and Abednego replied to the king, "O Nebuchadnezzar, we do not need to defend ourselves before you in this matter. If we are thrown into the blazing furnace, the God we serve is able to save us from it, and he will rescue us from your hand, O king. **But even if he does not,** we want you to know, O king, that we will not serve your gods or worship the image of gold you have set up." DANIEL 3:16-18

Why do bad things happen? And why do they happen to good people? Did you know that somebody asked Jesus this very question?

Now there were some present at that time who told Jesus about the Galileans whose blood Pilate had mixed with their sacrifices. Jesus answered, "Do you think that these Galileans were worse sinners than all the other Galileans because they suffered this way? I tell you, no! But unless you repent, you too will all perish. **Or those eighteen who died when the tower in Siloam fell on them—do you think they were more guilty than all the others living in Jerusalem?** I tell you, no! But unless you repent, you too will all perish." LUKE 13:1-5

Do you hear the underlying question here? "Why God? Why did this happen?" Maybe, just maybe, you could blame the Galileans. If they hadn't rebelled against the Romans, perhaps this terrible thing would not have happened to them. But Jesus takes it a step further when he reminds his listeners of the collapse of the tower in the wall of Jerusalem. Why did *that* happen? By chance, eighteen different people just happened to be in the tower when it fell. It was senseless and indiscriminate suffering.

Was it because they were worse sinners?

Or had less faith?

Or because God did it to judge them?

Or because the devil found a weak spot in their souls?

What Jesus *doesn't* say is perhaps as significant as what he does say. *Jesus, the Son of God, has the opportunity to answer the ageless, nagging question: "Why, God?" Yet Jesus, the Son of God, refuses to give the standard answers:*

It wasn't the devil.

It wasn't a question of the will of God.

And it certainly wasn't because those eighteen people were "worse sinners." Jesus flatly rules that one out.

I know this is really unsettling, but *Jesus doesn't answer the question.* And I am inclined to believe that if the Son of God has no simple answer, than I had better let it rest.

To me, that's the answer: Trusting God when there are no answers.

I think this is essentially what Jesus meant when he concluded: "Unless you repent, you too will all perish." In other words, life is fragile, and what matters most is not how well we can explain tragedy but whether or not we have a meaningful relationship with God. What matters most is not "why" it happened but where we go from here.

Why, God?
I don't know.
If I did, would it change how I feel?
Maybe there is no answer.
But Jesus is the solution.

Margie Dalton wrote to me:

One of the burning questions that haunts people who are grieving, or trying to cope with their tragedy and suffering, is, "Why?" Why God, when we prayed for protection? Why God, when the child was so young? Why God, at the prime of life? Why *now*?

There were times when I felt so wounded, so vulnerable, so cut to the core that all I could do was cling to the foot of the Cross, to hold on to Jesus, knowing that he was holding on to me when I started to lose my grip.

Words didn't help me a bit. What people said, and much of what I read, seemed so trite and irrelevant. My mind could not seem to grasp anything I read, and I was infuriated by those who informed me dispassionately, "It must be God's will, Margie."

Of course God allowed it, but *why*?

But Why?

I am convinced that the worst question any suffering Christian can ask is "Why?" It won't help to ask that, because God will never answer that question. The prophets, Peter said [see 1 Peter 1:10-12], told us about grace we would experience in troubled times. However, the prophets didn't have the foggiest notion of what they were talking about because they were in the dark. What God was up to was so marvelous that they couldn't begin to grasp it.

Even the angels want to inquire into what God is doing with you and me. They can't understand it either and are perplexed by the whole matter. If the angels can't figure it out, we puny humans shouldn't even try. Instead, we must by faith accept the fact that Christ is at work in our lives, even though it may not look like it.

DOUG MURREN[4]

I think these principles may be at the heart of Proverbs and Ecclesiastes and their unique positioning next to one another in the Old Testament. Proverbs is about how God is God when everything seems to be going our way. Ecclesiastes is about how God is still God even when it isn't. Both books were written by the same man, Solomon.

Proverbs is Hebrew wisdom literature, which is a sophisticated way of saying that it's a little bit like formula religion—simple statements about what works in life and what doesn't. Proverbs resonates with the theme, "Do good and you'll be blessed. And if you don't, you'll be cursed."

But I like to think about how Proverbs was probably written by Solomon when he was a younger man, when life was simple and he thought he had all the answers. In striking contrast, Ecclesiastes, written by Solomon when he was older, is a book of unanswered questions about the inconsistencies and injustices of life.

The book begins, "Meaningless! Meaningless!... Utterly meaningless! Everything is meaningless!" (Ecclesiastes 1:2) Yet looking straight into the eye of life's bewildering mysteries, Solomon concludes Ecclesiastes with the command, "Fear God and keep his commandments, for this is the whole duty of man" (12:13). In other words, whatever you make of the tragedies of life, what matters in the end is your relationship with God.

Can you believe that?

I once heard a pastor say that when he was young, he decided to write a book about how to raise children. As he got older, he was desperately looking for books on how to raise children. All of life is like that! Like Solomon, the older you get and the more you go through, the less sure you become about what it all means.

There are no easy answers, especially when your loved one dies. But there is always faith. Persistent faith in the face of great adversity. Job stood his ground, even though Satan had brought him to the brink of destruction. As Jesus told his disciples, we "should always pray and not give up" (Luke 18:1).

Fellow pastor and good friend Mark Buckley lost his oldest son in a tragic drowning accident a few years ago. Matthew did not die immediately, but was rushed to a local hospital where he was placed on life support. Mark's story of his son's death is one of faith and hope, even when hundreds of prayers were not answered:

It was the battle of our lives. I wept and pleaded with God. "Lord, we need young men like my son Matthew who will openly share the gospel with their friends! He's an A student. He's a virgin. He has never used drugs or been drunk. He has worked hard and honored his father and mother. Our nation needs men like him. We need Matt!"

Opening my Bible at random in the middle of the second night of our vigil, the first scripture I saw was Matthew 29:6, "*With God all things are possible.*" My heart leaped with hope. This was the same scripture that many friends had been quoting at the hospital.

On the third morning our doctors restated in the most clear terms the message they had been giving us from the beginning. "A person's brain is destroyed after four to five minutes when they are under the water and deprived of oxygen. Matthew was under the water for twenty minutes. His brain is devastated. Only a small portion of his brain stem is functioning. His chances for recovery from a medical perspective are zero. His only hope is for a miracle."

We thanked them for their honesty and assured them we believe in miracles. Though his body was barely functioning, his spirit was present. We anointed his feet with the tears of our intercessory prayers. Occasionally tears would come from Matt's eyes. It seemed like he could feel our pain. The elders of our church also anointed Matt with oil and prayed for his healing.

Our friends stood in faith beside us during the hours of our agony. They did not fear failure. They were not intimidated by the hospital environment. They did not pray half-heartedly, to cover themselves in case God did not heal Matt. They prayed with all their might. Matthew belonged to all of us.

During his last hours he began to breathe rapidly, like a runner nearing the end of a marathon. Kristina and I, along with our other children, stood around his bed. Several friends from our church and Matt's school were also present. We gathered at his bedside and watched him finish the race.

We all had one last chance to tell him how much we loved him. We thanked him for being a faithful son and a good buddy.

On October 6, 1975, at 1:14 A.M., Matthew was the first baby I ever watched come out of a mother's womb. On June 4, 1992, at 3:40 P.M., he was the first person I ever watched slip out of this world into the next. When he breathed his last breath, it seemed as if he crossed the finish line at the Olympics. I raised my hands and shouted in triumph, "He won the gold. He's a champion!"

We cannot bring our son back, but we are looking forward to the day we will join him in heaven.

Even in darkness light dawns for the upright…. His heart is secure, he will have no fear; **in the end** he will look in triumph on his foes. PSALMS 112:4, 8

Right now you're experiencing a terrible loss. It feels like you've lost the race. But in the end, you're going to win. "Weeping [and all your angry, unanswered questions and unsolved mysteries] may remain for a night, but rejoicing comes in the morning" (Psalms 30:5).

NOTES

ONE
More Questions Than Answers

1. C.S. Lewis, *A Grief Observed* (San Francisco: Harper & Row, 1961), 17-18.

2. Psalm 22:1; Matthew 27:46.

3. Richard Foster, *Prayer: Finding the Heart's True Home* (San Francisco: Harper San Francisco, 1992), 17-18, 24.

4. Helen Fitzgerald, *The Mourning Handbook: The Most Comprehensive Resource for Practical and Compassionate Advice on Coping with All Aspects of Death and Dying* (New York: Simon and Schuster, 1994), 74.

5. Lewis, 45-46.

6. Eugene Peterson, *The Message* (Colorado Springs: NavPress, 1993), 385.

TWO
Does Grief Come in Stages?

1. Fitzgerald, 74.

2. William Stringfellow, "The Joy of Mourning: On Grief and the Meaning of Resurrection" *Sojourners,* April, 1982, 29.

3. Earl A. Grollman, *Living When a Loved One Has Died,* 2nd ed. (Boston: Beacon, 1987), 15-17.

4. Arthur Freese, *Help for Your Grief* (New York: Schocken, 1977).

5. Gary Collins, *Christian Counseling: A Comprehensive Guide* (Waco, Texas: Word, 1980), 411-12, italics mine.

6. From Arthur Freese's discussion of the work of Erich Lindemann in *Help for Your Grief* (New York: Schocken Books, 1977), 20-21.

7. Freese, 20-21.

8. John A. Larsen, in *Baker Encyclopedia of Psychology*, David G. Benner, ed. (Grand Rapids, Mich.: Baker, 1985), 474.

9. Larsen, 473.

10. Freese, 24.

11. Freese, 7.

12. Margaret Stroebe, Wolfgang Stroebe, Robert O. Hansson, *Handbook of Bereavement: Theory, Research, and Intervention* (New York: Cambridge University Press, 1993).

13. Freese, 2.

THREE
I Can't Believe It!

1. Sheldon Vanauken, *A Severe Mercy* (New York: Bantam, 1981), 187.

2. Freese, 55-57.

3. Margie is simply expressing her personal opinion here. I'm not sure if this is true medically.

4. Lewis, 15.

5. Grollman, 22-23.

6. Helen Applegate, *Anchor in the Storm: Trusting God When It Hurts* (Seattle: Frontline Communications [Youth With A Mission], 1988), 95-96, first italics mine.

7. Applegate, 99-100.

FOUR
Why Are You So Afraid?

1. Billy Graham, *Facing Death: And the Life After* (Minneapolis: Grason, 1987), 55.

2. Graham, 49-50.

3. Ernest Becker, *The Denial of Death* (New York: Macmillan, 1973), 15.

4. John 11:25-26.

5. See Romans 3:10-18.

6. Grollman, 32-33.

7. Fitzgerald, 100.

8. Collins, 60.

9. Collins, 69.

10. Dale Simpson, "Anxiety," *Baker Encyclopedia of Psychology*, 67.

11. Collins, 67.

12. Lewis, 46.

13. 1 John 4:19, King James Version.

14. James Beck, *Why Worry?* (Grand Rapids, Mich.: Baker, 1994), 12.

15. Collins, 68.

16. Granger Westberg, *Good Grief: A Constructive Approach to the Problem of Loss* (Philadelphia: Fortress, 1961, 1972), 44-45.

17. Collins, 68.

18. Hannah Whitall Smith, *The God of All Comfort* (Chicago: Moody, 1956), 35.

FIVE
So You're Mad at God?

1. Grollman, 27.

2. Logan Jones, "A Pastoral Care Vignette: Silent Night," *Journal of Pastoral Care* 44 (Winter 1990): 399-400.

3. Robert L. Wise, *When There Is No Miracle* (Glendale, Calif.: Regal, 1977), 114-115.

4. Fitzgerald, 85-88.

5. Westberg, 50-51.

6. Frederick Buechner, *Wishful Thinking: A Theological ABC* (New York: Harper & Row, 1973), 2.

7. Grollman, 44-45.

8. Nicholas Wolterstorff, *Lament for a Son* (Grand Rapids, Mich.: Eerdmans, 1987), 15.

9. See Ephesians 6:10 ff.

10. J.B. Phillips, *The New Testament in Modern English* (New York: Macmillan, 1972).

SIX
Well-Meaning People, Witless Wisdom

1. Max Lucado, *In the Eye of the Storm* (Dallas: Word, 1991), 144-47.

2. Frederick Buechner, *Peculiar Treasures: A Biblical Who's Who* (New York: Harper & Row, 1979), 65.

3. Erin Linn, *I Know Just How You Feel: Avoid the Clichés of Grief* (Cary, Ill.: Publishers Mark, 1986), xii-xiii.

4. 1 Corinthians 4:14-15.

SEVEN
If Only I Had...

1. Grollman, 39-41.

2. Colin Brown, *Dictionary of New Testament Theology,* Vol. 1 (Grand Rapids, Mich.: Zondervan, 1975), 697-98.

3. Buechner, *Wishful Thinking,* 29.

4. Lewis Smedes, *Forgive and Forget* (San Francisco: Harper & Row, 1984), 29.

5. Philip Yancey, "Forgiveness is an unnatural act," *Christianity Today* (April 8, 1991), 36.

6. Sigmund Freud, as quoted in Yancey, 36.

7. J. M. Brandsma, "Forgiveness," *Baker Encyclopedia of Psychology,* 425.

8. Smedes, 151.

EIGHT
Memories

1. Grollman, 68-70.
2. Tony Martorana, "When Memories Bring Pain," *Charisma* (May 1995), 34-35.
3. Freese, 26, 62 ff.
4. Fitzgerald, 115-16, italics mine.

NINE
Saying Good-Bye

1. Leighton Ford, *Bible Illustrator for Windows*, 1994 [This is a computer program].

TEN
Sin and Death

1. Michael Simpson, *The Theology of Death and Eternal Life* (Notre Dame: Fides, 1971), 28-29.
2. Hans Küng, *Eternal Life* (New York: Crossroad, 1991), 160.
3. Küng, 162.
4. Graham, 41-42.
5. Grollman, 50.
6. D.A. Carson, *How Long, O Lord? Reflections on Suffering and Evil* (Grand Rapids, Mich.: Baker, 1990), 109.
7. As quoted in Sandra Bertman.
8. Raymond A. Moody, *Life After Life* (New York: Bantam, 1986), 12.
9. Luke 16:22.
10. Luke 23:43.
11. Diane Komp, *A Window to Heaven: When Children See Life in Death* (Grand Rapids, Mich.: Zondervan, 1992).
12. Komp, 40-41.
13. Timothy K. Jones, "Death in the Mirror," *Christianity Today* (June 24, 1991), 30.

14. Felix Salter, *Bambi* (New York: Simon and Schuster, 1928, 1969), 71-73.

15. Anonymous, "Letters to a Daughter: Clinging and Falling," *Christian Century* (October 26, 1994), 974-75.

16. Robert Morey, *Death and the Afterlife* (Minneapolis: Bethany, 1984), 40.

17. Jones, 31.

18. Verlyn Klinkenborg, "At the Edge of Eternity," *Life* (March 1992), 71.

19. Moody, 21-22.

20. Klinkenborg, 66.

21. Melvin Morse, *Closer to the Light: Learning from the Near-Death Experiences of Children* (New York: Ivy Books, 1991).

22. George Gallup, *Adventures in Immortality: A Look Beyond the Threshold of Death* (New York: McGraw/Hill, 1982), 11.

23. Moody, 88-93.

24. Klinkenborg, 71.

25. Melvin Morse, "Children of the Light," *Reader's Digest* (April 1991), 153.

ELEVEN
Heaven, Your Real Home

1. Loraine Boettner, *Immortality* (Phillipsburg, N.J.: Presbyterian and Reformed Publishing Co., 1956), 40.

2. Luke 23:43.

3. Morey, 94-95.

4. Graham, 220.

5. Joni Eareckson Tada, *Heaven: Your Real Home* (Grand Rapids, Mich.: Zondervan, 1995), 153-55.

6. Graham, 216-17.

TWELVE
Faith and Hope

1. Andrew Murray, *Absolute Surrender* (Chicago: Moody, N.D.), 94-96.

2. Lary Crabb, *Finding God* (Grand Rapids, Mich.: Zondervan, 1993), 86.

3. D. James Kennedy, *Delighting God: How to Live at the Center of God's Will* (Ann Arbor, Mich.: Servant, 1993), 55.

4. There is only one root term in the Greek for the word faith. New Testament Greek does not make a distinction between "belief," "believe," and "faith."

5. Ray Anderson, *Theology, Death and Dying* (New York: Blackwell, 1986), vi-vii.

6. Oswald Chambers, *My Utmost for His Highest* (Grand Rapids, Mich.: Discovery House, 1992), May 8.

7. Trevor Chandler, *Hope: The Answer to the Problem of Faith* (Kent, England: Sovereign World, 1993), 18.

8. Titus 2:13.

THIRTEEN
Unsolved Mysteries

1. Portions of this chapter have been adapted from my book *Overcoming the Dominion of Darkness: Personal Strategies for Spiritual Warfare* (Grand Rapids, Mich.: Baker/Chosen, 1990), 193-205.

2. *Bits and Pieces* (Vol. I, No. 6).

3. Theodor Herzl, as quoted in Rabbi Yechiel Eckstein, *What You Should Know about Jews and Judaism* (Waco: Word, 1994), 185.

4. Doug Murren, *Is It Real When It Doesn't Work?* (Nashville, Tenn.: Thomas Nelson, 1990), 38.

Other books of interest by Gary Kinnaman

Learning to Love the One You Married

When two people say "I do" they want it to last forever. But in these days of no-fault divorce and self-centered lifestyles, creating and sustaining a loving, committed marriage is not easy. In this biblically-based book, Gary Kinnaman pens a letter to his son and new daughter-in-law, giving them practical instruction that will help them, and other couples like them, succeed at marriage. $10.99

Angels Dark and Light

In this book, Gary Kinnaman provides a thoroughly biblical guide to the world of angels. He pulls back the curtain of this fascinating supernatural phenomenon, exploring the nature and purpose of these heavenly encounters. He answers popular questions surrounding angels and shares stories about ordinary people who have experienced angelic visitors. $10.99

Available at your local Christian bookstore
or from Servant Publications
PO Box 8617
Ann Arbor, Michigan 48107

Please include payment plus $3.25 per book
for shipping and handling.